Pleasure Zones

Space, Place, and Society
John Rennie Short, *Series Editor*

PLEASURE

Bodies, Cities, Spaces

ZONES

David Bell

Jon Binnie

Ruth Holliday

Robyn Longhurst

&

Robin Peace

SYRACUSE UNIVERSITY PRESS

First Edition 2001
01   02   03   04   05   06   6   5   4   3   2   1

The paper used in this publication meets the minimum requirements of
American National Standard for Information Sciences—Permanence of
Paper for Printed Library Materials, ANSI Z39.48–1984. ∞™

Library of Congress Cataloging-in-Publication Data
Pleasure zones : bodies, cities, spaces / David Bell . . . [et al.].— 1st. ed.
p. cm. — (Space, place, and society)
Includes bibliographical references and index.
ISBN 0-8156-2897-8 (alk. paper) — ISBN 0-8156-2898-6 (pbk. : alk. paper)
1. Body, Human—Social aspects. 2. Sex role. 3. Gender identity. 4. Human geography.
5. Personal space. 6. Public spaces. I. Bell, David, 1965- II. Series.
GN298.P54 2001
306.4—dc21   2001020956

Contents

David Bell teaches cultural studies at Staffordshire University. He is coeditor of *Mapping Desire* (1995), *The Cybercultures Reader* (2000), and *City Visions* (2000), and coauthor of *Consuming Geographies* (1997) and *The Sexual Citizen* (2000).

Jon Binnie lectures in human geography at Manchester Metropolitan University. His work has appeared in *Society and Space, Gender, Place, and Culture, Environment and Planning,* and *Progress in Human Geography.* He is currently writing a book on sexuality and globalization, *Globalizing Desires,* and is coauthor of *The Sexual Citizen* (2000).

Ruth Holliday lectures in cultural studies at Staffordshire University. She is coeditor of *Organization/Representation* (1998), *Organizing the Body* (2000), and *Contested Bodies* (2001). She recently completed an Economic and Social Research Council-funded project entitled *Public Performances, Private Lives: Identity at Work, Rest, and Play,* from which the material in her chapter is drawn.

Robyn Longhurst is a lecturer in the Department of Geography, University of Waikato. She has published essays in numerous edited collections and geographical journals and is author of *Bodies: Exploring Fluid Boundaries* (2001).

Robin Peace is currently a senior researcher for the Ministry of Social Policy, New Zealand. She was previously a lecturer in feminist geography at the University of Waikato.

Upstairs/Downstairs—
Place Matters, Bodies Matter

Jon Binnie, Robyn Longhurst, & Robin Peace

The essays collected together in this volume are about bodies and spaces, reflecting the academy's growing interest in the interrelationships between space, place, body, and identity. Over the last two decades, geographers have begun to recognize the body as a politicized site of struggle and contestation. Internationally, social scientists have given considerable attention to the body and the ways it is linked to space and place. A significant dimension to this emerging work on the body has been a focus on sexual identities and communities. In this respect, David Bell and Gill Valentine argue that in the 1990s "sexuality is—at last—finding a voice as a legitimate and significant area for geographical research" (1995a, 11). Coupled with this specific focus on sexuality, a more general interest in the politics of embodiment in geographical research is also emerging. This field of study recognizes the body as a vehicle for understanding the relationships between people and place (see, for example, Ainley 1998; Duncan 1996; Nast and Pile 1998; Pile 1996).

Geographers have also come to recognize that the materiality of bodies is constricted by gender, sex, sexuality, race, class, nationality, and disability. For example, Louise Johnson (1989) and Linda McDowell (1995) examine gendered bodily performances in the workplace; Michael Dorn and Glenda Laws (1994) focus on medicalized bodies; Peter Jackson (1994) discusses representations of black men's bodies in advertising; and Isabel Dyck (1995) examines women with multiple sclerosis. As postrationalist, postcolonialist, and poststructuralist perspectives gain both popularity and recognition within the social sciences, the body, in its discursive and material forms, is fast becoming a key area of research.

Before we proceed, however, a few points of clarification seem in order. We want to define here, albeit contingently, some of the core working concepts at the heart of *Pleasure Zones*. The first of these concepts is *the body*. Although we have acknowledged the emerging work in geography (and elsewhere) that looks at the body, the question "What is a body?" remains difficult to answer. We all have one or are one, but the term *body* cannot be contained within a tidy dictionary definition (Longhurst 1997)—something always seeps through. Perhaps this is not surprising given that we use our bodies in complex ways. Bodies are sites of identity, morality, aesthetics, action, work, play, pleasure, pain. Our bodies have a materiality, a "thingness"—bones, flesh, organs, nerves, muscles, and blood. This materiality, however, is always constituted within discourse. Geographers such as Heidi Nast and Steve Pile (1998) have made the important point that bodies are also always constituted within place.

Western thought has long assumed a duality of mind and body, an assumption established at least since the Enlightenment. Feminist theorists such as Moira Gatens (1996) and Elizabeth Grosz (1994) have argued convincingly that this mind/body dualism is gendered: the mind is correlated with terms considered positive, such as *consciousness, rationality,* and *masculinity,* whereas the body has been associated with terms considered negative, such as *nonconsciousness, irrationality,* and *femininity.* Critical theorists have also pointed out that bodies are not universal bedrocks; there is no *"the body";* rather, *bodies* have racial, cultural, age, class, gender, and sexual specificities. They have particular capacities and desires that are structured by hegemonic and normative practice. However, theorists have unpacked this normativity, revealing that bodily expressions of identity, such as gender and sexuality, are not natural but *naturalized.*

For example, in her influential book *Gender Trouble,* Judith Butler argues that gender is "The repeated stylization of the body, a set of repeated acts within a highly rigid frame that congeal over time to produce the appearance of substance, of a natural sort of being" (1990, 33). Elaborating on this definition, Butler goes on to suggest that "Acts, gestures, enactments, generally construed, are *performative* in the sense that the essence or identity that they otherwise purport to express are *fabrications* manufactured and sustained through corporeal signs and other discursive means" (1990, 136, emphasis in original). Gender is thus something that we "do," and do recurrently. Moreover, Butler displaces the heteronormative alignment of gender and sex by arguing that the gendered body is performative, explaining that "It has no ontological status apart from the various acts which constitute its reality. . . . [I]f that reality is fabricated as an interior essence, that very interiority is an effect and function of a decidedly public and social discourse" (1990, 136). Repeated performances of expected behaviors, then, establish regulatory practices for gendered, sexed, and sexualized bodies—and these practices are, importantly, imprinted on space (Bell et al. 1994). One such regulatory practice is heterosexuality. Heterosexuality constitutes an unmarked category in Western culture and as such has been subject to rigorous critique and deconstruction for more than a decade. A great deal of this critique has been produced under the label *queer.*

In *A Feminist Glossary of Human Geography* (1999), McDowell and Sharp note that "queer is a complex term having multiple origins and meanings" (225). Bell and Valentine explain further: "Queer has become a notoriously indefinable watchword for certain so-called radical theoretical and activist stances in 1990s sexual politics, the first of which was arguably the act of reclaiming the very word 'queer' from its use as homophobic slang to be a label used *by* a variety of sexual dissidents" (Bell and Valentine 1995a, 20, emphasis in original). In an attempt to define *queer,* Bell and Valentine quote from a pamphlet circulating in New York in the early 1990s entitled *I Hate Straights:* " 'Being queer means leading a different sort of life. It's not about the mainstream, profit margins, patriotism, patriarchy or being assimilated. It's not about being executive directors, privilege and elitism. It's about being on the margins, defining ourselves; it's about genderfuck and secrets, what's beneath the belt and deep inside the heart; it's about the night' " (Bell and Valentine 1995a, 20).

Bell and Valentine note that queer politics emerged at a particular historical juncture when numerous governments failed to respond adequately to the AIDS crisis and a great deal of anti-"gay" legislation was put forward, particularly by "new right" administrations, especially in the United Kingdom and the United States (see also Bell and Binnie 2000). Existing political strategies were proving impotent for lesbians and gays, so "a new adversarial politics was needed; it was time for queers to bash back" (Bell and Valentine 1995a, 21).

Queer politics are closely linked to queer theory—a diverse body of critical literature often seen as having emerged out of gay and lesbian literary criticism, particularly the work of Eve Kosofsky Sedgwick (1990). This theory is most commonly situated within postmodern and poststructuralist frameworks. A key concern of queer theorists is the disruption and deconstruction of binary oppositions such as heterosexual/homosexual and gender/sex (Butler 1993).

Geographers have made effective use of queer theory and politics to further our understandings of the performance of sexual identities in space. Bell, Binnie, Cream, and Valentine (1994), for example, use Butler's work to examine the construction of public space as heteronormative. More recently, geographical knowledge has itself been subjected to queer readings (see Binnie 1997a and 1997b; Binnie and Valentine 1999).

We hope that this discussion has clarified the kinds of positions from which the essays in this volume have been written; it is now time to tell another story—the story of how this book came about and where we're writing from.

Connections

This book stems from cooperation between writers from the United Kingdom and Aotearoa/New Zealand. David Bell and Jon Binnie first met Robyn Longhurst at the annual meeting of the Association of American Geographers in San Francisco in 1994, and Jon first met Robin Peace at the Regional Conference of the International Geographical Union in Prague the same year. Discussions about the book continued when David and Jon met Robin at a Social and Cultural Geography Study Group reading weekend in Hebden Bridge, England, in 1995 and during Jon's sabbatical stay at Waikato University in 1996. When Ruth Holliday joined the cultural studies staff at Staffordshire University and came to know Jon through David, there seemed to be an ideal opportunity arising out of this network to bring together each writer's insights into the body-place relationship. Through these intellectual and institutional links, we have built up certain commonalities in terms of our own particular perspectives on developments within feminist and cultural geography, and on the way both the body and sexuality have become incorporated into geographical (and other) research agendas.

In terms of similarities, we found that at the time we were among a very small number of geographers concerned with the politics of the body. In this sense, we felt isolated from the heartland of contemporary human geography. We shared a frustration with the ways in which even the "new cultural geography" and feminist geography regarded the bodily as outside of geographical knowledge—as reflected in Robyn Longhurst's statement that the body is geography's "Other" (1997). However, times have changed, and as we come to the finishing stages of pulling this book together, it now appears that the body has been at the center, not the periphery, of geographical knowledge, given the recent avalanche of publication in this area.

There are, however, significant gaps in this evolving literature. What is missing, in particular, are commentaries on the "politics of pleasure." The literature on the geographies of the body and sexuality has little talk of amusement, comfort, happiness, delight, or delectation. Yet *pleasure* is so ultimately inseparable from embodiment. For example, despite its title, Paul Rodaway's 1994 book *Sensuous Geographies* includes little to arouse any sense of pleasure (see Bell 1996). Clearly, the abstractions of theorizing the body frequently leave little room for discussion of what having a body feels like (see also Holliday and Hassard 2000). However, there are exceptions, such as Lynda Johnston's 1996 study of female bodybuilders, who speak of their desire for the ultimate "built body." The participants in her study discuss their pains *and* pleasures in sculpting their sinews. We should be clear, however: we do not agree that any discussion of pleasure must uncritically celebrate pleasure for pleasure's sake—this is not banal cultural populism inscribed on body theory—but merely want to note that geography as a discipline has been notably reluctant in studying pleasure other than as a clean-cut, pure psychoanalytical conception of desire. Pleasure, as a crucial part of the materiality of embodiment, deserves serious, critical (but also pleasurable) attention.

Geographers from Aotearoa/New Zealand have begun to express their frustration with being situated in the theoretical periphery of geographical knowledge and with writers from the Northern Hemisphere who tend to dictate the pace of developments in the subject and ignore the different ways of doing geography found elsewhere. For example, in a guest editorial entitled "American Unlimited" in *Environment and Planning D: Society and Space,* Larry Berg and Robin Kearns relate the story of a rejection letter one of them received from the editor of an American geographical journal stating that the paper's "focus on New Zealand is limiting." "The editor's comments are ironic because the idea that 'geography matters' . . . has become almost axiomatic in social geographic thought over the past decade" (1998, 128). Commenting on the self-declared Anglo-American bent of Ron Johnston's *Geography and Geographers* (1997), Berg and Kearns argue that "Although geographers from the 'peripheries' are allowed to participate in such debates, they are rarely able to set the agenda or frame the epistemological boundaries. Geography's 'conceptual space' is thus constituted in highly ethnocentric terms" (1998, 129).

Berg and Kearns suggest that writers from Australia and Aotearoa/New Zealand occupy a paradoxical space in being "between identities as coloniser and colonised," as Meaghan Morris puts it (1992, 471; qtd. in Berg and Kearns 1998, 129). Although the contributors to this book share Berg and Kearns's concerns, we feel that the particular marginality we occupy in terms of the subject matter we research and write about means that we need transnational cooperation, but this cooperation is hampered by the sheer physical distance that separates us.

Producing this book has been a pleasurable experience in many ways, but this pleasure has been constituted by its binary opposite—pain. The physical distance between the authors, some working from "up over" (United Kingdom) and others working from "down under" (Aotearoa/New Zealand) at times proved painful as the disembodied texts of e-mail did not convey all that we wanted, despite all the cyberhype. This is, of course, the case with any book coauthored by people who do not live and work in the same location, but the problems in putting this book together seemed to be compounded by the fact that we were working on topics still commonly regarded as at best frivolous and not worthy of serious academic consideration or at worst dirty and contaminating.

This status possibly opened up the potential for each of us to feel more acute isolation within our respective academic institutions. It was ironic that each of us was writing on bodies, desire, sex, pleasure, fun, and so on, and yet the realities of our own lives across different sides of the world were often structured by difficulties that we faced in universities with a long history of dichotomizing and valuing the mind over the body, straight over queer, seriousness over amusement.

Each contributor to this book also shares a frustration with traditional Marxist theory, which too often marginalizes the bodily and the queer, and sees them as external to or excessive of knowledge production—including geographical knowledge production. Against this view, we all acknowledge the need to both queer the social and socialize the queer (see also Bell and Binnie 2000) and are keen to find ways to bring together queer theory, social and cultural theory, and geographical knowledge (cf., Maynard 1999). Each chapter in this volume embodies these concerns and seeks in very different ways to articulate social as well as spatial formations of the bodily and the queer. Indeed, the strength of the book lies in the very different approaches each author has taken to the subject; it is our intention that these chapters be read against as well as alongside one another. For example, one major theme running through a number of the chapters is the materiality of the sexed body, but this theme is thought about and worked with in different ways. Longhurst's and Binnie's chapters, for instance, deal with it very differently: Longhurst's ethnographic study versus Binnie's more textual approach. Each author has written about the limits of representation in creating embodied geographies, and these chapters also demonstrate certain limitations in creating embodied geographies as distinct from geographies of the body.

Longhurst's chapter provides a detailed empirical study of the links between body and place in terms of the management of space and identity among pregnant women in Hamilton, New Zealand. Her work directly addresses the messy materiality of the sexed body, as opposed to less-"threatening" work on *discourses* of the body. Although asserting that there is no such thing as a body outside of social and cultural discourses, Longhurst's chapter acknowledges that embodied geographies should not shy away from discussing the physicality of the body and its fluids, as well as the *experience* of that materiality.

Peace's chapter takes issue with the concept of the "missing lesbian" in geographical knowledge. Peace deploys Julia Kristeva's notion of abjection to examine the marginal status of lesbians within the geographical canon. She challenges this marginality and considers the ways in which the lesbian has been reconfigured in the evolving literature on lesbian geographies; this approach is significant for contextualizing work on sexuality and space through a consideration of gender and equally for contextualizing work in feminist geography through a consideration of sexuality. As Sally Munt (1995, 1996) has shown, the lesbian body configures a particular spatiality, to which geographical research must respond.

Holliday's chapter examines the ways in which queer identities are expressed on the surfaces of bodies—which Peace has also discussed in terms of "marking up" the lesbian body. In particular, Holliday focuses on clothing and the ways in which clothing is used in accounts of the construction and expression of self-identity. The chapter is based on a research project on performativity and management of identities in the spaces of work, home, and leisure. The research uses video diaries in order to capture performative and textual configurations of the body. One key notion that emerges in Holliday's work is the way that performances of identity are naturalized through the language of "comfort." The chapter argues that "subcultural" discourses of comfort draw mainly on essentialism. Through discussion of her empirical material, Holliday argues that a social poststructuralist politics of the self is necessary to move the subject beyond the recourse to essentialism and individualism.

In contrast to the earlier chapters, Bell's essay focuses in on gay men's identity and urban space. The chapter provides a critical and utopian overview of work on the sexualized city. The section on "gay bars as straight places" poses the question of economic colonization: Is the visibility of queerness (both to other queers and to the straight community) more economically motivated in terms of straight colonization rather than in terms of queer emancipation? In other words, are the new gay bars spaces for the consumption of queerness as commodity rather than for the emancipation, liberation, and promotion of queerness? Also, as a corrective to work that emphasizes the most visible aspects of urban gay life (sites of public sex, consumption spaces, gentrified neighborhoods), Bell focuses on the sexualization of domestic space in his discussion of "sodomy in suburbia" and on the lives of rural lesbians and gay men.

Following on from David Bell's chapter on sexuality and the city, Jon Binnie examines the limits and possibilities for realizing the materiality of sex in the city. Discussing the relationships between taste, morality, and aesthetics, Binnie poses the questions: What is distinctive about desire in the city? Do cities foster or create specific pleasures? Through a reading of the sadomasochist's use of urban space and a consideration of the erotics of the city provided in the pulp-splatter fiction of Stewart Home, Binnie asks that we consider representation and materiality as coterminous elements in the articulation of the body-city-space relationship.

Each of these chapters constitutes a particular challenge to the disembodied nature of geographical knowledge. Moreover, each contributor to the book is keen to reassert the value of the social and the material in theorizing about embodiment and queer identities. *Pleasure Zones*, then, signals a reorientation in work on sexuality, space, and embodiment—one that maintains the political imperative of previous work but is not troubled by combining that imperative with pleasure.

Pleasure Zones

1

Trim, Taut, Terrific, and Pregnant

Robyn Longhurst

In this chapter, I examine pregnant bodies and the public spaces they occupy in relation to sport. Iris Marion Young argues that neither philosophers nor feminists have given nearly enough attention to conceptual and normative issues about women's relation to sport (1988, 335). Geographers, also, have paid scant attention to women's relation to sport, especially to understanding sport as "a site through which questions related to social and political power, domination, ideology, agency, and transformative possibilities must be considered" (Cole 1994, 5). Pregnant women's relationship to sport has received even less coverage in academic literatures.

I draw on the experiences of thirty-one women who live in Hamilton, Aotearoa/New Zealand[1] and were pregnant for the first time.[2] Hamilton is

An earlier version of part of the second half of this chapter appeared in R. Longhurst, "Discursive Constraints on Pregnant Women's Participation in Sport," *New Zealand Geographer* 51, no. 1 (1995): 13–15. I would like to thank the editor of *New Zealand Geographer* for permission to reproduce this material. Also, parts of the section entitled "Out of Shape" have been published in R. Longhurst, *Bodies: Exploring Fluid Boundaries* (London: Routledge, 2001). I would like to thank Routledge for permission to reproduce this material.

1. *Aotearoa* is the Māori term for what is commonly known as New Zealand. Over the last decade, especially since 1987 when the Māori Language Act was passed making Māori an official language, the term *Aotearoa* has been used increasingly by various individuals and groups. For example, all government ministries and departments now have Māori names, which are used on all documents in conjunction with their English names. Despite these moves, however, the naming of place is a contestatory process (see Berg and Kearns 1998), and I use the term *Aotearoa/New Zealand* in an attempt to highlight this contestation.

2. The pregnant women involved in the study ranged in age between sixteen and "older than thirty-five." Their personal incomes ranged from "nil" to "NZ$40,001–50,000 per year."

a city of 132,000 people (Census of Population and Dwellings 1996) located to the west in the northern half of the North Island of Aotearoa/New Zealand. The city grew as a service center for the outlying rural Waikato dairy industry and has a reputation for being rather "conservative." Over a period of two years—from 1992 to 1994—I carried out participant observation, focus groups, and in-depth interviews in order to gain a greater understanding of pregnant women's experiences of public space. It became evident during the study that many of these pregnant women tended to withdraw from public places associated with pleasure—such as nightclubs, bars, pubs, restaurants, cafés. They also tended to withdraw from public activities such as sport, especially sport that requires a high and sustained level of performance—for example, skiing, running, rugby, tramping, and so on.

The aim of this chapter is to examine why many of the pregnant women whom I interviewed tended to withdraw from sport. I do so by first addressing the question "What is a pregnant body?" Second, I address the question "What is sport?" Third, I examine the bodies of the thirty-one participants as sites of struggle, making reference to some of the regulatory regimes that pregnant women are subject to in relation to sport in Hamilton, Aotearoa/New Zealand. Finally, I argue that pregnant bodies in Hamilton are constructed as potentially dangerous, ugly, large, and leaking, whereas the female "sporting body" tends to be represented as hard, athletic, trim, and flexible. It is here that a tension exists for women who are pregnant but also want to engage in sport.

What Is a Pregnant Body?

Julia Cream poses two riddles:

RIDDLE 1
We all have one.
Most of us wish we had a different one.
What is it?
The body

Four of the participants defined themselves as New Zealand Māori. The other twenty-seven participants defined themselves as New Zealand European or Pākehā.

RIDDLE 2
Most of us acquire it at birth.
Some change it, others play with it.
What is it?
xǝS
(1995, 30)

Cream claims that there are not any simple answers to the composite of her two riddles: "What is the sexed body?" Sexed bodies are not simply there, ready and waiting examination. I use Cream's work as the starting point of this chapter because, like the sexed body, the pregnant body is problematic. It is not possible simply to add pregnancy to a body, nor is it possible simply to add a body to something called pregnancy. Likewise, it is not possible simply to add something called "sport" to a pregnant body. Pregnant bodies, like all bodies, are an interface between politics and nature, and between mind and matter. They are "real," but at the same time they are socially constructed. "Real," material pregnant bodies do not exist outside of the political, economic, cultural, and social realms. They require examination and explanation: they are "not a starting point" (Cream 1995, 31). Like all bodies, pregnant bodies are "already a constructed and particularised view of nature" (Eisenstein 1988, 91, cited in Cream 1995, 31). Therefore, pregnant bodies cannot be assumed to be "fixed, coherent, and stable" (Cream 1995, 32). They are not "an irreducible sign of the natural, the given, the unquestionable" (Kuhn 1988, 16, cited in Cream 1995, 32).

Bodies, and in this instance pregnant bodies, therefore, possess "no pure, uncoded state, outside the realm of culture" (Fuss 1989, cited in Cream 1995, 33). Perhaps the most prominent exponent of this approach to embodiment is Michel Foucault (1977, 1980, 1985, 1986). Foucault's emphasis on embodiment allows consideration of not only how discourses and practices create subjects but also how these practices construct certain sorts of bodies with particular kinds of power and (in)capacities. In particular, Foucault focuses attention on the ways in which bodies are disciplined through various social and political regimes (see especially Foucault 1977).

Approaches such as Foucault's allow us to begin to make sense of speaking of bodies as having a history.

> If the body is granted a history then traditional associations between the
> female body and the domestic sphere and the male body and the public

sphere can be acknowledged as historical realities, which have historical
effects, without resorting to biological essentialism. The present capacities
of female bodies are, by and large, very different to the present capacities
of male bodies. It is important to create the means of articulating the historical realities of sexual difference without thereby reifying these differences. Rather, what is required is an account of the ways in which the
typical spheres of movement of men and women and their respective activities construct and recreate particular kinds of body to perform particular kinds of task. (Gatens 1992, 130)

If the historical effects of the ways in which power constructs bodies are to
be understood and challenged, it is necessary to examine the typical
spheres of movement of men and women in their respective activities and
in the places they occupy. For example, the bodies of pregnant women living in Hamilton in 1992 are constructed and inscribed in ways that are different from the bodies of pregnant women who live in the United States of
America or from the bodies of pregnant women who lived in Hamilton
thirty years ago. During the course of this research, I spoke with a sixty-
year-old woman, Carol, who had been pregnant while living in Hamilton
in 1962. She explained that during the early 1960s women in Hamilton, including herself, wore maternity corsets that laced up the back "like great
big shoe laces." Carol claimed that these corsets were not comfortable, but
pregnant women wore them because it was widely believed that they sup-
ported the back. "They seemed to think that the back took a lot of strain in
those days when you were pregnant." The discourses about pregnant
women's backs has changed in the intervening years. Currently, although
it is still widely accepted that some pregnant women suffer from backache,
corsets are not advised. It is now commonly believed that the baby's position in the womb can cause backache for the pregnant woman. The advice
in the 1990s is to perform specific exercises in an attempt to shift the baby's
position or to do gentle stretching exercises that may relieve the ache.

    People such as Dunden (1991), Foucault (1980), Gallagher and
Laqueur (1987), and Laqueur (1990) have documented the history of the
sexed body, but there is still limited work on *pregnant* bodies as temporally
and spatially differentiated. One useful account of an attempt to locate
pregnant bodies within a temporal context, however, is that by Carol
Brooks Gardner (1994). Using literary sources, mainly advice manuals and
medical writing, Gardner demonstrates that in the United States in the

nineteenth century the physical state and the social situation of pregnancy was used to explain physical and mental traits considered undesirable in children. Work of this type, though, is still rare.

In short, it is vital to understand the social place of pregnant embodiment—that is, to understand the biology of pregnant bodies as historically and culturally located. Pregnant bodies are not simply sets of biomedical facts that science is gradually uncovering (see Morgan and Scott 1993, 7–10). What it means to be pregnant shifts across time and space.

Consider, for example, Carlo the pregnant man.

Pregnant Man Thrilled to Be Giving Birth
"Carlo" the pregnant man is about to give birth—probably next month.

The 32-year-old male nurse, who his Philippines' doctors say is six months pregnant, is an hermaphrodite born with both male and female organs.

The man, whose name has not been made public but who has been given the nickname Carlo, says he is thrilled and delighted about the prospect of motherhood. *(Waikato Times,* May 27, 1992, 1)

Pregnant bodies make sense only within specific temporal and geographical contexts. Carlo the pregnant man who is looking forward to motherhood is not (yet) intelligible to most of us. It completely disturbs our notions of pregnant embodiment if men can become pregnant. In the movie *Junior,* Arnold Schwarzenegger plays the part of a pregnant man. A number of reviews of the movie claimed that women tended to find it humorous, but men found it less appealing (more threatening?). New biotechnologies—such as cloning, sex selection, surrogacy, ectogenesis, and gene manipulation—mean that pregnant bodies (and perhaps in the future these bodies will increasingly be "male" bodies) are a site of continual negotiation and contestation.

Given the proliferation of new reproductive technologies in Westernized regions (see Hepburn 1992 on technologies in Australia) over the last decade, it is perhaps intelligible, to some at least, that eggs can be taken from a woman, fertilized with her partner's sperm, and implanted in the woman's mother—in other words, that a grandmother can carry her own grandchild in her womb. Yet this scenario too seems on the border of the ways in which most of us understand pregnant embodiment.[3]

It is also possible for "virginal" (read in this instance: someone who has not had heterosexual intercourse with penile penetration) women (men?) to become pregnant. Many people believe that the Virgin Mary—the mother of Jesus Christ—conceived solely by the direct intervention of the Holy Spirit so that Mary remained miraculously a virgin during and after Christ's birth. The pregnant virgin is historically and culturally specific—that is, her body is intelligible only in specific contexts.

More recently, the virginal pregnant woman tends to be culturally intelligible in contexts where reproductive technology is available and where it is socially and politically permissible for such women to have access to this technology or to find means of their own in order to achieve conception. In recent years, for example, an increasing number of lesbian women have chosen to bear children (Kenney and Tash 1993, 119). Although some may have heterosexual intercourse in order to conceive, others may choose different methods, such as inserting a donation of sperm from a friend into their own vagina with a syringe. Currently in Aotearoa/New Zealand, there are debates about who ought to have rights to fertility treatment because there are no guidelines or legislation governing these rights. At the moment, the industry rather than national policy regulates and controls the fertility industry. Dr. Richard Fisher of Fertility Associates claims that currently he and his colleagues are expected to "play God" in deciding who is to be treated and who is not (Television New Zealand, Channel 3 News, July 11, 1994). Fisher is aiming to prompt public awareness about this issue in the hope of building "community consensus" about who ought to receive treatment.

According to the Human Rights Commission and a ministerial advisory committee on assisted reproductive technologies, access to infertility treatments should be available regardless of sexual orientation, age, and marital status. However, the first survey of public opinion on the issue shows that the public disagree. Although 86 percent of respondents believe that the new birth techniques should be available to infertile couples who are married, only 24 percent think these same techniques ought to be available to lesbian couples, and only 17 percent think they ought be available

3. A family who did this was interviewed on *The Oprah Winfrey Show*, which screened in New Zealand in 1993. The response from the studio audience was, by and large, puzzlement.

to heterosexual couples where the woman is past menopause (see *Listener* 1995, 14–15).

Like the new reproductive technologies, fetal or in utero surgery is also culturally and historically (un)intelligible. Prior to the 1980s, it would have made little sense to most people. Likewise, it may seem absurd to people who do not live in places where high-technology obstetrics is the norm. The most dramatic type of fetal surgery involves the actual removal of the fetus from the uterus with its return upon completion of the surgery (Blank 1992, 116). One example of an application of this procedure was conducted to repair a diaphragmatic hernia on a twenty-four-week-old fetus (Harrison, Adzick, and Longaker 1990). In considering the question of what a pregnant body is, it is interesting to ponder whether a woman (or man?) is still pregnant when the fetus is being operated on and is not in her (his?) womb.

It is also interesting to ponder the notion of being pregnant and dead. The best-documented case of postmortem pregnancy to date involved eighteen-year-old West German Marion Ploch, who died in a car accident in October 1992 (Middleton 1996, 22). Germany was polarized by the decision to keep the four-months-pregnant woman on life support until her child—dubbed "Frankenstein's baby" by the media—reached full term. In Aotearoa/New Zealand, twenty-year-old Megan Garrett died in a car accident on December 30, 1995. Doctors delivered her son on January 2, 1996 (Middleton 1996, 18). There have also been several cases in which women have asked medical (and legal) "authorities" to inseminate them with the sperm of their dead partners.

It is also interesting to examine a new linguistic term currently in vogue in Aotearoa/New Zealand. A semantic shift appears to have occurred from "I'm pregnant" to "We're pregnant." In an interview, Joanna Paul, who was a leading presenter of one of Aotearoa/New Zealand's prime-time current affairs programs, recalls her experience of telling her partner that she was pregnant: "Matt said what is wrong? I said, I . . . ah . . . we're . . . pregnant" (*New Spirit*, August 1994, 4, ellipses in original). In the same article, the interviewer claims, "In fact when Joanna talks about being pregnant, the term 'we're pregnant' crops up quite a bit." Two of the women involved in my research also used the phrase "we're pregnant."

What does it mean for two bodies to be pregnant with the same fetus? Is it the same thing for a lesbian couple to be pregnant as it is for a heterosexual couple to be pregnant? When men make claims to pregnancy by way of saying "we're pregnant" (and I have heard several men use this phrase), does it serve to increase or reduce their partners' sense of empowerment during pregnancy? Does the sharing of pregnant embodiment undermine pregnant women's bodily autonomy? If "we" are pregnant, then presumably will "we" end up having a caesarean section? Has a politics of equality led to the eradication of any recognition of sexually embodied difference?

The idea that "we" (read: two individuals) can be pregnant with the same fetus is given credence in the practice of the couvade. Men, in many areas of the world, but especially in Amazonia, ritually imitate and experience aspects of pregnancy and giving birth. Jeremy MacClancy explains:

> Like their pregnant partners, they may give up their normal routine activities, observe the same prenatal restrictions, and keep to the same food taboos. In the most dramatic examples, they retire to their hammocks and simulate labour pangs. This seemingly cranky conduct is often explained by members of those cultures as being a paternal attempt to aid the spiritual development of the otherwise vulnerable newborn babe. Without the mother there is no child, without the father's contribution the child may not survive. (1993, 86)

When a colleague told me he had experienced morning sickness during the early months of his wife's pregnancy, I began to question whether a cultural equivalent to the behavior in Amazonia exists in Western societies. It seems that since the 1960s doctors in England and Sweden have recognized a particular set of symptoms shown by almost 20 percent of their pregnant patients' male partners. MacClancy claims:

> Men afflicted by this "couvade syndrome" tend to be quite strongly attached to their mother, to have lost their virginity relatively late in life, and to be older (on average over thirty) and to have older parents than nonsufferers. Also, their female partners often become anxious about the impending birth within the first months of their pregnancy. These wretched men can suffer morning sickness, gastro-intestinal problems, and toothache; they may gain weight, become irritable, complain of lack of sleep, or even start to lactate. (1983, 86)

Another interesting facet of pregnant embodiment is phantom pregnancy. Occasionally Western women exhibit many of the signs of pregnancy (at least those signs specific to Western cultures, such as tiredness, morning sickness, tenderness of the breasts, and perhaps even a swelling of the abdomen), yet they are medically diagnosed as *not* pregnant. Such pregnancies are termed *phantom pregnancies:* a woman may experience the sensations associated with having a fetus in her womb, but the fetus is an illusion, immaterial. Is the woman who holds the specter of a fetus within her body and who experiences many of the psychological and physiological changes usually associated with pregnancy indeed pregnant? And, if not, why not? Such questions have no easy answers.

The question "What is pregnant embodiment?" is made even more difficult to answer by considering *cultural difference.*[4] A consideration of cultural difference is perhaps one of the most obvious ways to attempt to understand how the biological body exists for the subject only through the mediation of a web of cultural and social images of pregnant embodiment. I am not suggesting here that the materiality of all pregnant bodies remains the same while perceptions simply change. The body and mind cannot be separated. Varying historical and cultural understandings literally make different bodies. Take, for example, the understandings of pregnancy of Māori[5] and Pākehā[6] women in Aotearoa/New Zealand.

It is difficult, and not always useful, to generalize about Māori women's experiences and understandings of *hapūtanga*[7] because they are a diverse group occupying varying socioeconomic positions within specific *hapū*[8] and *iwi.*[9] In general, however, Māori women who are pregnant are

4. Bhabha defines the term *cultural difference* as "the process of the *enunciation* of culture as 'knowledge*able,*' authoritative, adequate to the construction of systems of cultural identification" (1994, 34, emphasis in original).

5. *Māori* is the term commonly used to refer to the *tangata whenua* (literally "people of the land") or indigenous peoples in Aotearoa/New Zealand. I use this term here but wish to problematize such use. As Spoonley points out, "the word 'Maori' is really a convenience for Pākehā to lump together divergent groups" (1993, xiii).

6. In this research, the term *Pākehā* refers to Aotearoa/New Zealand-born people of European descent. Although the term *Pākehā* has been (and at times still is) highly contested in Aotearoa/New Zealand (see Larner and Spoonley forthcoming; Spoonley 1993), it is now used as a standard term of classification of ethnicity in the New Zealand Census.

7. *Hapūtanga*—frequently referred to simply as *hapū*—is the Māori word for pregnancy.

8. In this instance, *hapū* refers to subtribe, but as noted above, the word also means "pregnant."

9. *Iwi* can refer to bone, people, and strength, but in this instance I am referring to tribe.

still today sometimes considered *tapu*.[10] Many Māori women, however, "choose" to adopt, or at least are subject to, mainstream (read: hegemonic/Westernized) maternity procedures and protocols. In Aotearoa/New Zealand, it is common for Pākehā women and many Māori women to understand pregnancy through Westernized biomedical models.

What I have done in this section is explain some of the ways in which pregnant embodiment is a complex interweave of nature and culture. The question "What is pregnant embodiment?" can be answered only by temporally and spatially locating pregnant bodies. Pregnant bodies are not the same everywhere. Biology cannot be ignored, but nor can it be treated as an unproblematic bedrock of human existence. It is for this reason that I have chosen to examine pregnant embodiment as it exists within one specific place and time and in relation to one specific activity: thirty-one pregnant women's relationship to sport as it exists in Hamilton, Aotearoa/New Zealand, 1992–94.

Sport—"A Notoriously Slippery Concept"

Iris Young claims that "Sport is a notoriously slippery concept" (1988, 336). I agree. It is not a term that is easy to define, but for the purposes of this chapter I attempt at least some partial definition. The *Collins English Dictionary* (1979) defines *sport* as "an individual or group activity pursued for exercise or pleasure, often involving the testing of physical capabilities and taking the form of a competitive game such as football, tennis, etc." According to this definition, then, attending horse or greyhound race meetings, being a tourist, or having sex are sport because they are "individual or group activities pursued for exercise or pleasure." This definition is somewhat broader than I intend. Iris Young adopts a slightly narrower definition of sport by including bodily capacities and skills. She states: "whatever else it is or is not . . . sport is the achievement of a non-utilitarian objective through engagement of bodily capacities and/or skills" (1988, 336). Presumably, however, Young's definition of sport could also include activities such as walking, bicycling, dancing, swimming in the surf, working on getting a suntan, or climbing trees. For the purposes of this discussion, I adopt a still narrower definition.

10. Something is in a *tapu* state when it is under the influence of the *atua* (god or spirit). Its opposite is *noa*, or not under the influence of the gods or spirits (see Hanson 1982, 344).

I discuss only those sports that require a high and sustained level of performance. I do not include what are sometimes referred to as fitness or leisure activities. What I am calling high-performance sports are usually outdoor activities. In Aotearoa/New Zealand, the most common high-performance outdoor sports are fishing, cycling, tramping, sailing, jogging, and hunting *(New Zealand Official 1996 Year Book* 1996, 274). Others, more masculinized, are archery, pistol/rifle shooting, boxing, fishing, mountaineering, wrestling, fencing, martial arts, motor boating, motorcycling, trail biking, mountain biking, orienteering, rowing, and skateboarding. None of the participants in my study mentioned these very masculinized sports. In this chapter, I make reference to the sports they did mention—jogging, touch rugby,[11] scuba diving, skiing, and "backyard" cricket.

My reasons for focusing on what I am calling high-performance sport are twofold. First, the women with whom I spoke tended not necessarily to withdraw from exercise or leisure—for example, going for walks or swimming in a pool—but they did withdraw from high-performance sport. It is useful for the purposes of this chapter, therefore, to examine the different constructions of female bodies in relation to pregnancy and high-performance sport. Such sports tend to be coded as "masculine" and therefore as unsuitable for pregnant women.

Second, high-performance sport plays an important role in the construction of national identity in Aotearoa/New Zealand. "Fifty four percent of New Zealanders participate in at least one outdoor activity per month; 36 percent participate regularly" *(New Zealand Official 1996 Year Book* 1996, 303). Sports such as tramping, skiing, white-water rafting, alpine climbing, fishing (sports that are commonly thought to reflect New Zealand's frontier past) are often considered to be integral to the lives of most New Zealand men as well as of many New Zealand women. "The 1880s in New Zealand witnessed the growing demand for the right of women and girls to unrestricted physical development and the beginning of female participation in institutionalized forms of recreation" (Crawford

11. Although in Aotearoa/New Zealand Rugby League and Rugby Union serve as a *rite de passage* for many men, touch rugby is often played by "mixed" teams—men and women. In touch rugby, the ball must be placed on the ground when a player is touched rather than tackled. The game has become increasingly popular in Aotearoa/New Zealand over the last five years.

1987, 166). The *New Zealand Official 1996 Year Book* states: "For many New Zealanders the successful New Zealand sportsman or woman represents the archetype of the battler succeeding against the odds" (1995, 301).

Scott Crawford argues that Aotearoa/New Zealand is a country devoted to sport and that the sport image has been an important foundation for the development of a "national identity" (1987, 161). Sporting success in Aotearoa/New Zealand is seen to forge national pride and is "the most valued form of cultural achievement" (Crawford 1987, 161). The *New Zealand Official 1996 Year Book* states: "Sport, fitness and leisure have played an important part in creating and shaping New Zealand's national image, both at home and abroad, and contribute much to the lifestyle New Zealanders enjoy. In New Zealand there is the potential for everyone to participate in some form of sport or leisure activity and it is government policy to promote access to it for all New Zealanders" (269).

It is because high-performance (outdoor) sport plays such an integral role in people's identity in Aotearoa/New Zealand that I wish to examine it in relation to the production of "different" discursive and material constructions of pregnant women's bodies.

Pregnant Bodies: Sites of Struggle over Sport

For many years, pregnant women in Aotearoa/New Zealand have been advised against engaging in sport or "strenuous exercise" because it might harm the fetus. A number of advice manuals—such as those by Champion and O'Neill (1993); Mittelmark, Wisswell, and Drinkwater (1991); and Peterson (1994)—indicate the "dos and don'ts" of sport for pregnant women. These manuals indicate that for a long time it was considered undesirable and of substantial risk to the baby for pregnant women to combine sport and pregnancy. For example, in a 1953 book written by the New Zealand Obstetrical and Gynaecological Society, entitled *The Expectant Mother,* it is advised that "Strenuous activities are to be condemned. Those which should be avoided are swimming, cycling, horseback riding, golf, tennis, violent movements and jolts, running, lifting heavy weights and hurrying up and down stairs" (34). The society adds to this advice, however: "housework is not harmful." This statement about housework indicates pregnant women were not being advised to avoid certain movements, such as hurrying, bending, stretching, and lifting per se, but rather that they were not to perform these movements in public places. Housework most certainly involves bending, stretching, and lifting, and yet it was sanctioned in the privacy of the home. Only "strenuous activities" in public places were "to be condemned."

Exercise during pregnancy, on the other hand, is heralded as having the potential to offer a number of benefits to women. These benefits include maintaining and even improving fitness; preventing excessive weight gain; and reducing problems associated with pregnancy, such as leg cramps, constipation, and low back pain (see Wilson 1994). Despite these supposed advantages of exercise during pregnancy, most of the pregnant women who took part in this study gradually withdrew from sport requiring high levels of sustained energy—for example, touch rugby, diving, climbing, skiing, and running.

Sandy, who was between fifteen and nineteen years old and twenty-six-weeks pregnant, commented: "I used to do a lot of running, but I've stopped the running because I just think the pounding and all that isn't very good" (individual interview).[12] When Paula found out that she was pregnant, she stopped going to the gym immediately, despite having just paid fees for a new membership. "I just joined again and then I found out I was pregnant, so [laughter] the membership didn't lapse but the attendance did. . . . It was actually only a three-month subscription so it wasn't too bad. . . . I didn't really lose that much on it [laughter]. Um, I will definitely go back after the baby's born though; um, it's probably best not to start trying to get active at this stage of the pregnancy" (in-depth case study). When I asked Dorothy, whose baby was due on the day of our interview, if her lifestyle had changed since she had become pregnant, her response was: "Well, for a start, I'm a lot less active. I was a regular sort of

12. The choice of transcription system is closely related to the type of analysis being attempted. As Ochs (1979) points out, transcription is already a form of analysis. It is simply not coherent to speak of the accuracy or completeness of a transcript without some frame for deciding what sorts of features of conversation or talk are relevant or valued and what can be ignored (see Cook 1990). The conventions that I use are as follows. The starts of overlap in talk are marked by a double oblique (//). Pauses were not timed, but simply marked with a period within parentheses—(.). Omitted material is marked with standard ellipses. Note also that although speech "errors" and particles (for example, *err, ummm*) that are not full words are included, I have added commas, full stops, question marks, and exclamation marks in a manner designed to improve the readability of the extracts while conveying their sense, as heard, as effectively as possible. Words or particles said with particular emphasis are italicized.

person at the gym when I got pregnant, and loved my sports, but I've stopped going to the gym altogether" (individual interview). As these women became increasingly visibly pregnant, their behaviors in relation to sport as well as in relation to many other activities in their lives became increasingly surveyed (see Foucault 1977)—both in covert and overt ways—by loved ones, friends, and strangers. Pregnant women are often watched in an attempt to ensure that they take care of themselves, but more importantly that they take care of their unborn child.

An example of what I consider to be rather extreme surveillance is reported by Cheryl Cole (1994), who discusses the mandatory pregnancy testing of female athletes in the United States.

> Mandatory pregnancy testing became the topic of debate during the spring of 1992, when Gary Torgeson, the coach of the women's softball team at California State University at Northridge, suspected that a player was pregnant, despite her insistence to the contrary. Torgeson argued that he was concerned about her pregnancy because "harm could come to her and her baby" because the woman was a pitcher (a high-risk behaviour by Torgeson's view). Torgeson appealed to the NCAA's mandatory and routine drug-testing policy in an effort to legitimate his call for mandatory pregnancy testing (Torgeson 1992). (Cole 1994, 22)

Consider also the following example: in this conversation, Denise and Kerry are trying to decide whether they will continue to play touch rugby now that they are both pregnant (at the time of this conversation Denise was eight-weeks and Kerry sixteen-weeks pregnant). The spectators' surveillance in this instance worked effectively in monitoring Denise and Kerry's behaviors.

> ROBYN: Are you going to keep playing [touch rugby]?
> DENISE: (.) No. I'll see, yeah, see how I feel. I'll probably go in tonight for a little bit, but . . . yeah, I fell, it wasn't last week I fell over, it was the week before, wasn't it?
> KERRY: The week before, yeah.
> DENISE: I didn't really think anything of it. I just got up. But everyone that was on the sideline went *Oh!* And I just got up and someone that was behind me said, "Oh, are you all right?" and I said "yes." I just got up and carried on and didn't really think anything of it. A lot of people say "a trip

can be quite bad, you know, a miscarriage, if you trip over or something like that." (joint in-depth case study)

The public response "Oh" to Denise's tripping over acted, at least in part, to discourage both Denise and Kerry from continuing to play touch rugby even though Denise herself did not regard her tripping over as a problem. There may have been many complex reasons for each of them choosing to stop playing, but undoubtedly the public response to their playing was one of the determining factors.

The response to Paula's playing cricket when she was twenty-weeks pregnant was similar, although, on this occasion it was Paula's husband, rather than a crowd of people on the side-line, who acted to dissuade her.

> PAULA: I still get out and play cricket with the guys and stuff now [laughter]. David says I'm not allowed to run after the ball, I have to walk after it [laughter]. . . . My brother was batting, and he hit the ball, and it went miles off, and I raced after it, and he goes, David was going, "Paula walk, Paula don't do that" [laughter]. (in-depth case study)

Clearly Paula is contesting the boundaries of what is considered appropriate behavior for a pregnant women. Although she modifies her playing of the sport (by walking after the ball), she continues to be involved in the game despite friends and family's protestations.

Michelle also contested the boundaries of what is considered "appropriate" behavior for a pregnant woman. She remained fit and extremely physically active throughout her pregnancy (mainly through dance, which could be considered in this instance to be high-performance sport). Michelle, however, was forced to deal with negative responses to her continuing high level of exercise. She told a story about filling in to teach a dance class for a colleague.

> MICHELLE: I showed up to take one of his classes one day, and he just started ranting about ballet dancers he had known who had miscarriages because they had carried on dancing, you know, he ranted at Sally [Michelle's employer], "I don't want her in the class," so I just ranted back that this was something between my doctor and myself, and it was none of his business. (individual interview)

Pregnant women may contest some discourses in some instances in their lives, but may comply with hegemonic constructions of pregnancy in other instances. For example, Michelle explained that although she has kept dancing, she has given up skiing since becoming pregnant: "That was the only time I've felt really down about being pregnant. Here am I looking pretty big, and he had a couple of students . . . she and a friend who had been Miss Somewhere or something quite beautiful, arrived at the door with their skis to pick up *my* husband, and here was I, 'Bye, dear,' sitting with my feet up feeling like a moron" (individual interview). A number of other research participants who usually skied as part of their winter recreation had also given up skiing since becoming pregnant.

> DAWN: I can't go skiing this year.
> ROBYN: Oh! You are a skier?
> DAWN: Yeah, we were planning to go to the South Island, but . . . then I think oh well, better not, I'm only pregnant once. (//)
> ANGELA (//) We probably would've gone skiing too. Not that we go every year, but we sort of go a couple of times a season.
> ROBYN: Is it fear of hurting the baby that stops you going, that you might fall?
> DAWN: (.) Yeah, I guess. It depends what stage you're at though [Dawn was twenty-nine-weeks pregnant], yeah, like if you, I think it's that you're not supposed to anyway, probably because the height you know anyway. Something to do with the oxygen level.
> ANGELA: Oh really!
> ROBYN: The altitude?
> DAWN: I've heard that anyway. (focus group)

The supposed "truth" of this claim about the "oxygen level" is not what is at issue in relation to the particular argument being mounted in this chapter. Rather, what is important here is that the information that Dawn had heard or read (from whatever sources) was enough to stop her from skiing during pregnancy without further question, illustrating the powerful role that stories or discourses play in relation to producing behaviors. Although none of the pregnant women interviewed skied at any stage during their pregnancy, a male interviewee, Dan, explained that his partner, Tracy, had skied during pregnancy. "Most of the time I was really pleased that my partner was skiing . . . but as time went on it did start to concern me. . . . I remember I had a streak of thinking how *irresponsible* of her" (individual interview, emphasis added).

Expectations to be a good mother are put on women not just after the baby is born, but also during pregnancy and sometimes even before pregnancy. They are advised that if they want to get pregnant, then they should adopt a healthy diet, must be fit (but not "too active"), must not smoke, and so on. The "becoming mother" must follow prescribed behaviors; to transgress these norms is to risk the well-being of her fetus (who in the eyes of many already has full or at least protohuman status) and to be labeled as "irresponsible."

Scuba diving is another sport mentioned by a research participant as being off-limits. Mary Anne, an international travel consultant, who was thirty-six-weeks pregnant at the time of the interview, explained that "You are not allowed to dive at all once you know you are pregnant. It can cause problems. I stopped doing any sport quite a long time ago. I had a bit of bleeding, and the doctor said I shouldn't do anything" (individual interview).

Wilson claims that "active women have . . . been reported to have higher self-esteem and improved mental outlook during pregnancy" (1994, n.p.). Perhaps it is worth hypothesizing at this point that high self-esteem may not be so much an effect of exercising during pregnancy, but rather that only those women who have high self-esteem are prepared to contest the boundaries of "appropriate" behaviors for pregnant women. High self-esteem is necessary to contest the surveillance and the many discursive constraints that operate to keep exercise/sports and the Pregnant Woman in mutually exclusive conceptual categories.

Although the thirty-one women with whom I spoke did not radically contest the boundaries of what tends to be considered acceptable behavior in relation to sport, some women do continue their involvement in sport during pregnancy. One of the best examples is Alison Hargreaves of England, who climbed the North Face of the Eiger when she was six-months pregnant. A route was named after the event, "Fetus on the Eiger" at Stanage Edge (Osius 1993, 168). Yet women, such as Hargreaves, who push the boundaries of what are widely considered acceptable behaviors for pregnant women are frequently forced to face what might be considered negative consequences. For example, there was a bitter public outcry from both climbers and the general public in response to Hargreaves's climbing the

Eiger when she was six-months pregnant. Alison Osius, who climbed until near the end of her pregnancy, reports: "After I belayed Mike Benge, my husband, I stepped up to second the climb, harness riding low and chalk-bag belt high, both meeting in the back. The whole cliff went silent. (Paranoiac, I imagined vibes: 'She shouldn't be doing that.')" (1993, 168).

Despite the fact that the general advice that health professionals offer to pregnant women on exercise and sport today is usually to carry on, the long-held belief of earlier times that almost anything except lying in bed (alone, of course) might bring on bleeding, abortion, or premature labor has not totally disappeared. Although women have now demonstrated that sport can continue during pregnancy, many activities are still considered far too dangerous for pregnant women. It is widely believed that a pregnant woman's primary concern ought to be for her fetus and that for this child she must sacrifice all and risk nothing.

Pregnant women are often considered primarily not as subjects in their own right but as containers or vessels for unborn children. Young argues, "Pregnancy does not belong to the woman herself. It is a state of the developing fetus, for which the woman is a container; or it is an objective, observable process coming under scientific scrutiny, or it becomes objectified by the woman herself as a 'condition' in which she must 'take care of herself' " (1990c, 160). The process of pregnancy can undermine women's subjectivity. The well-being of the fetus is often prioritized, which is significant in that it could be argued that engaging in high-performance sport affords women the status of "body subject" rather than "body object." Iris Young explains that women in general are often excluded from sport because sport exhibits "body-subjects" and women in Western cultures are defined as "body-objects" (1988, 335). This distinction makes it conceptually difficult (impossible?) for women to engage in sport because their bodies cannot simply switch from being socially coded as objects to being subjects. It follows, therefore, that if women participate in sport, either they are not "really" women, or the sport they engage in is not "really" a sport.

It is useful to examine this idea in relation to pregnant women. Given that pregnant women clearly are women who are fulfilling the role that "real" women have always fulfilled—the bearing of children—then the sport they engage in must not "really" be a sport. For example, the one physical activity that most pregnant women seem to continue on with, and even to take up during pregnancy, is walking. But of course, walking is not usually defined as a sport.

The normalizing of pregnant women's behaviors, therefore, occurs not only to protect the fetus but to protect the masculinism of particular sports. After all, what does it say about touch rugby if pregnant women can play it? Would pregnant women's very presence in the game serve to problematize the notion that sporting prowess is naturally masculine? In other words, what I am arguing is that it is not the institutions and practices of sport that necessarily exclude pregnant women (for example, gyms or rugby clubs do not state explicitly that they will not accept memberships from pregnant women), but rather that pregnant women are excluded from the very idea or notion of sport.

It is imperative, therefore, to examine some of the discourses that inhabit the pregnant body. Understanding manifestations of power relations in the context of pregnant women's personal material histories may allow for the demonstration of the fluidity of the circumscribed boundaries set by social relations as they are lived in and through bodies.

Out of Shape

Cheryl Cole suggests sport is "expressed in the everyday normalizing practices of remaking bodies, identities, and pleasures" (1994, 6). Today, female bodies involved in high-performance sport tend to be part of a "new feminine aesthetic—versatile, athletic, hard and slick" (Cole 1994, 16). They represent "a new dimension in the historical-cultural map of gender body-styles, the health/beauty/exercise complex, and commodity production" (Cole 1994, 16). Pregnant women, on the other hand, tend to be discursively constructed as large, fat, unable to bend or stretch; sometimes they are even represented as "disabled." Pregnant bodies do not possess clear firm boundaries, but rather they continually threaten to split their one self into two (possibly more). It is in this regard that understanding abjection may be useful.

Young claims that understanding abjection enhances "an understanding of a body aesthetic that defines some groups as ugly or fearsome and produces aversive reactions in relation to members of those groups" (1990b, 145). She states that "Racism, sexism, homophobia, ageism and ableism are partly structured by abjection, an involuntary, unconscious judgement of ugliness and loathing" (1990b, 145). Abjection is the affect or feeling of anxiety, loathing, and disgust that the subject has in encountering certain matter, images, and fantasies—the horrible—to which it can respond only with aversion, with nausea and distraction. Kristeva (1982) argues that the abject provokes fear and disgust because it exposes the border between self and other. This border is fragile. The abject threatens to dissolve the subject by dissolving the border. The abject is also fascinating, however, seeming to draw the subject in order to repel it (see Young 1990b, 145). Grosz, in discussing Kristeva's work on abjection, claims: "The abject is what of the body falls away from it while remaining irreducible to the subject/object and inside/outside oppositions. The abject necessarily partakes of both polarized terms but cannot be clearly identified with either" (1994, 192).

The abject is undecidable both inside and outside. Kristeva uses the example of "disgust at the skin of milk" (Grosz 1989, 74)—a skin that represents the subject's own skin and the boundary between it and the environment. Abjection signals the tenuous grasp "the subject has over its identity and bodily boundaries, the ever-present possibility of sliding back into the corporeal abyss out of which it was formed" (E. Wright 1992, 198). In ingesting objects into itself or expelling objects from itself, the subject can never be distinct from the objects. These ingested/expelled objects are neither part of the body nor separate from it. The abject (including tears, saliva, feces, urine, vomit, mucus—but also the fetus/baby, "waters," colostrum, breast milk, afterbirth) marks bodily sites/sights that will later "become erotogenic zones" (mouth, eyes, anus, nose, genitals) (Grosz 1989, 72; see also Wright 1992, 198).

Young uses the notion of abjection in order to argue that some groups become constructed as "ugly" (1990b, 142). In this section, I build on Young's notion by examining the possibility that pregnant bodies are sometimes constructed as ugly, both by pregnant women themselves and by others. This construction becomes particularly evident when considering pregnant women's involvement in sport. The abject, like the pregnant body, is neither subject nor object. The abject exemplifies the impossible, ambiguous, and untenable identity of each. It is not surprising, therefore, that some work that links pregnancy and abjection has been written. Kelly Oliver (1993), for example, in *Reading Kristeva* discusses "the abject mother." Jan Pilgrim (n.d.) uses Kristeva's concept of the abject to examine representations of the naked pregnant body.

It is my contention that pregnant women, at least in part, occupy the status of "despised, ugly, and fearful bodies" (Young 1990b, 142; see also Longhurst 2001)—perhaps even grotesque. Given that sport is so often considered to be the domain of the "body beautifuls" (not everyone wants to wear shorts in public!), it is perhaps not surprising that most of the pregnant women in this study tended to withdraw from sport.

Representations of the pregnant body as ugly were also evident among the research participants' accounts of pregnancy. Katie, a woman in her midthirties, explained, "I didn't swim as much at the beach this year. That's partly 'cause I couldn't be bothered and partly because I felt like a whale." Roy described his wife Paula as being "40/40/40 statistic range." Paula responded that she was looking forward to going to the gym after the baby was born and "getting a body back." Jude feared being ridiculed about her pregnant body. She commented: I never wrote a diary as a child in case somebody that I didn't want to found it, and I think it would be the same with a photo [of me pregnant]. Somebody would be leaving through my album and laugh. Somebody that I didn't want to see me like that." When Dorothy was thirty-four-weeks pregnant, she was advised by a female colleague that she no long fitted the [sleek?] corporate Auckland image and that she ought to stop work and go home.

One of Kerry's male colleagues described the ultrasound scan to her in the following way: "For fifteen to twenty minutes you lie there with all this gel all over you with your *guts sticking out*" (emphasis added). Clearly his use of the phrase "guts sticking out" to describe Kerry's pregnant stomach is interesting in that it does nothing to indicate the attractiveness of her stomach—rather, to the contrary. Another male colleague informed Kerry after she had spilled a cup of tea on herself, "When you start breast-feeding, you'll have more stains than that over your body probably. . . . A good tip is to use your husband's hankies and put them down you." Yet again, the comments indicate a body that leaks and that will be covered in unwanted bodily fluids—stains—that will need to be controlled.

Members of groups subject to oppression "often exhibit symptoms of fear, aversion, or devaluation towards themselves and toward members of their own groups" (Young 1990b, 147). In relation to pregnant embodiment, it is useful to examine the words and phrases not only others but also pregnant women themselves use to discuss the bodies of pregnant women and their own embodiment. Images of fatness, disability, incapacitation, discomfort, and ugliness are abundant.

"We were gonna park in the disabled car park," said Denise. Denise's statement draws a correlation between being pregnant and being disabled. Christine claimed: "People sometimes treat you like you're just about handicapped when you're pregnant." Ngahuia, although much less directly, also drew a correlation between being pregnant and being disabled. "I use the paraplegic toilets" she said.

Pregnant women often discussed their perceptions of their bodies when I asked whether they had any photographs of themselves pregnant. When I asked Mary Anne, who was thirty-six-weeks pregnant at the time of the interview, this question, she replied: "*No,* and I don't intend to have any. . . . I don't want anyone to look at my big bum. I don't mind my body shape of the baby; it's my hips and thighs that I don't like the thought of [anyone] looking at" (individual interview). Jude, a university student who was thirty-three-weeks pregnant, responded similarly to the same question. "I never wrote a diary as a child in case somebody that I didn't want to found it, and I think it would be the same with a photo. Somebody would be leafing through my album and laugh. Somebody that I didn't want to see me like that" (individual interview).

The judgments others pass on pregnant women's bodies may lead to their feeling uncomfortable about their own bodies. For example, Terry's mother-in-law left Terry feeling as though she "couldn't win."

She [her mother-in-law] would cook this nice dinner, and you'd have to eat it all up to please her. . . . there's always this constant thing with her every time she sees you. "Oh, are you eating enough?" and I'd say "Oh yes." I'd say, "Oh look, you should see how much I've been eating, look at this weight I've put on," and then she'd say, "Oh, oh dear, I think you should be exercising." You know, and you think "you can't win." And then she'd say "Look . . . [Terry,] I think you're too big, you know. Look at—'cause her daughter is ten weeks further on pregnant than I am and she's put on the same amount of weight as me—she's really put on very little for how far along she is. And I've found that really difficult, and then I'd go around say to the daughter's place, and she'd say "Oh gosh, look at you, you've put a lot of weight on your face haven't you?" [laughter]. And you end up, you know, you're self conscious enough about it.

MARGARET: Yeah, you are, it makes it worse I think.

TERRY: I would actually probably not have thought about it unless she'd said something about it. And then I went to my doctor, and I said, "Have I got on too much weight?" I said, "You know, my mother-in-law says I'm too big, you know." And I got really paranoid about it.

MARGARET: I did at first too about it.

TERRY: Yeah, I found that quite difficult, especially like in the last two weeks I've put on a kilo each week, you see, and I think, "Oh I've put on ten already, and I'm twenty-five weeks, so what am I going to be like at the end?" (focus group)

One of the topics of conversation that tended to lead women to talking about their pregnant bodies was swimming and swimwear. General practitioners often advise pregnant women that swimming can be a useful activity to pursue in order to keep healthy. Yet it is seldom made explicit that swimming usually involves pregnant women revealing their new body shape in public. Given that many pregnant women dress in baggy garments that act to disguise their swelling stomach—"you do cover up your pregnancy. You always wear big clothes that are bigger than your tummy," said Jude—it comes as no surprise that many feel uncomfortable wearing a swimming costume and even decide not to swim.

ADRIENNE: I was a bit embarrassed the first time I went swimming. I sort of thought—oh, you know! But it was comforting to see other pregnant women there . . . 'cause people tend to accept that when they see more pregnant women there—it's all right. . . . the very first day I went there wasn't a pregnant women in sight. I went in the afternoon, and there wasn't a pregnant women in sight, and you feel as if the whole world is watching you.

JOAN: When I was about five months . . . we went swimming, I was swimming in the pool, but lots of the girls, because I wasn't that big, had bigger tummies than I did anyway, so it didn't bother me at all, but I don't think I would swim now. I'm too uncomfortable—people looking at me.

MOIRA: I went swimming yesterday at Te Rapa pools. It doesn't really worry me, only that Dave [the interviewee's husband] works there, and so I'm maybe a bit more self-conscious because they know me, rather than if I just didn't know anybody there I probably wouldn't worry as much. (focus group)

None of the visibly pregnant women whom I interviewed wore or had considered wearing bikinis while swimming in public (although a number of them had worn bikinis prior to pregnancy). Yet it was evident that women who did swim when pregnant faced problems in obtaining swimwear that fit them comfortably.

DAWN: I actually bought some maternity togs because they were on special [sale]. . . . they are really expensive. I tried on a normal pair, and they just didn't feel right.

ANGELA: I just loaned a pair [of maternity togs] off a friend yesterday that are black so that is quite good, covers me up a bit. I probably wouldn't wear black togs if I wasn't pregnant. (focus group)

There is an uneasiness about the public exposure of pregnant bodies, which makes it unlikely that pregnant women will want to "expose" themselves in sports clothing—shorts, singlets, leotards, fitting bicycle shorts, swimwear, and so on. Often, both the pregnant woman herself and those who view her experience this uneasiness about the exposure of pregnant bodies. Howard (Christine's husband) talked about his response to seeing pregnant women on beaches.

I've been to a lot of beaches . . . and I've seen pregnant women in all sorts of states of dress and undress, and it seems quite a normal, ordinary course of events. Yet it is different. . . . I guess something in me tells me that a pregnant woman is somehow in a different status to a nonpregnant woman, in a way a pregnant woman is sort of nonsexual, outside of courtship rules. In the meat market, beaches do feel like that sometimes; there are lots of participants who are not involved in the game, for instance families and pregnant women. (individual interview)

Howard raises an important point. Pregnant women are often perceived as being "outside of courtship rules"; they are constructed as "nonsexual" beings despite the fact that at the same time they are clearly marked as having been sexually active. Yet once a woman is pregnant, she is often considered to be no longer sexually available, active, or desirable, even though her own desires may have increased. Young argues that the pregnant woman's "male partner, if she has one, may decline to share in her sexuality, and her physician may advise her to restrict sexual activity. To the degree that a woman derives a sense of self-worth from looking 'sexy' in the manner promoted by dominant cultural images [in Hamilton the dominant culture defines feminine beauty as slim] she may experience her pregnant body as being ugly, and alien" (1990c, 166). Constructions of the pregnant body as ugly, alien, and not "sexy" or sexual help to explain why the pregnant body is so often considered to be private and that it ought not to be engaged publicly in sport. "Sexual politics" permeate sport. Longhurst and Johnston claim that women bodybuilders frequently reported feeling more sexually attractive.

> LYNDA: Do you feel more sexually attractive?
> JENNY: When I wear my leotard at the gym Barry [her husband] says "Gosh all these guys are always looking at you when you wear that leotard." Yeah it's quite a dag yeah um yeah I think a lot more people sort of notice you when you are lot more shapely. (individual interview)

Another research participant, Sarah, claimed: "It [body-building] makes me feel much more sexually attractive." Fiona also felt she had become more sexually attractive: "Yes definitely. . . . Makes me feel much more sexually attractive" (individual interview, Longhurst and Johnston forthcoming).

Whether men experience pregnant bodies as ugly, fearful, and abject to a greater degree than women is difficult to determine. There is little doubt that women are in no way exempt from feeling abjection toward the pregnant body, but according to some of the research participants' comments it is possible that men may find the uncontainable, seeping corporeal more difficult to "deal with." Rebecca, who was older than thirty-five, explained that not only was her husband going to accompany her during the labor and birth, but so too was a woman friend. Rebecca explained, "I've got a husband that's a bit panicky," and "he'll probably faint." The friend's presence was for her husband's sake—"it's for Stewart"—rather than for her own. Another research participant, Katie, whom I spoke with again after her birth, reported that her husband had fainted during the labor. He fainted not at the moment of the birth itself, but when Katie was receiving an epidural injection in her back.

Kerry explained that when watching a video at antenatal class of a woman whose waters had broken and who was going into labor, one of the husbands had to leave the room—"he was being sick."

> KERRY: Yeah, he walked out.
> DENISE: One of the fathers watching it?
> KERRY: Yeah [laughter] he was gone [laughter] . . .
> DENISE: He's gonna be a lot of use, isn't he? Carl won't like those videos.
> KERRY: It does, it puts them off. (joint in-depth case study)

Later on in the same class, the pregnant women and their husbands were informed that during labor the pregnant woman could have a bowel motion. On their way home from the class, Kerry's husband said to her, "I hope you don't shit yourself." Kerry responded by saying that if she did, he couldn't blame her. "It'd be horrible," her husband responded. Kerry's husband was disgusted by the prospect of what Kerry's body might do.

Yet it was not only men who responded to and constructed the pregnant body as ugly, fearful, and abject. There may well be some differences between men's and women's responses to the pregnant body—men may be more afraid than women of the body that threatens to seep and split its one self into two—but most of the women themselves also constructed their pregnant bodies as ugly.

Although some respondents did report feeling good about the baby kicking and about a sense of fascination concerning their changing body shape, most of the comments about their corporeality were negative. In fact, of the thirty-one pregnant women with whom I spoke, only two reported feeling really positive about their body shape. Perhaps it is not surprising that one of these participants, Michelle, continued to dance professionally throughout her pregnancy. "A pregnant body is really quite beautiful, it is just the feeling of, I don't know, it's like I feel good about being pregnant. One of the really nice things is I've got breasts. I was always one of these flat-chested people, and so I feel so voluptuous during pregnancy" (individual interview). In response to the question "How do you feel about your pregnant body?" Ngahuia, the university lecturer, replied: "I love it. I think it's good to have a positive attitude about it because so many women get put off by the fact that being pregnant means your body changes and you look awful, but let's face it, it is natural to look like that when you are pregnant, and it's good to have a positive attitude and to set positive examples to other women to encourage them" (individual interview).

Although these accounts of pregnant embodiment might apply in similar ways to all women who are pregnant, at the same time the group of thirty-one women with whom I spoke represent only "one slice" (Young 1990b, 141) of the oppressions of racism, sexism, homophobia, ageism, and ableism. The accounts I have offered attempt to explain how pregnant women in Hamilton in 1992–94 became culturally defined as abject bodies, which dissuaded them from engaging in sport.

I did not collect accounts of women's postnatal experiences of sport, but most women who had engaged in sport prior to pregnancy expressed some desire to return to their particular sport after giving birth and thereby "get back into shape." The slogan "Get your body in shape" was used by a fitness center and broadcast on a commercial radio station in Hamilton, Aotearoa/New Zealand, in October 1995. The advertisers unproblematically assumed that during pregnancy or prior to slimming, the body in question is out of shape or perhaps has no shape. But what does it actually mean for a body to not be in shape? Obviously, the advertisers took for granted the desirability of a *specific* body shape. Paula said that she would "definitely go back [to working out at the gym] after the baby is born." Many pregnant women seem to desire to return to their pre-pregnant corporeal form. The slogan "Become Some Body" was used to advertise the Les Mills Sports Spectrum on national television in Aotearoa/New Zealand throughout 1995. The advertisers played on the ambiguity of becoming "some body" in terms of both corporeality and subjectivity. The message that the advertisers wanted consumers to read from this slogan is that working out at the Sports Spectrum would enable them to craft their corporeal self in such a way as to command respect—self-respect and the respect of others. Becoming a member of the Sports Spectrum would enable them to become "some body" rather than remain a "no body." The question about how anyone can have "no body" in the first instance is not posed. Most pregnant women in the study desired to return to sport, thereby "Becoming Some Body" after their baby had been born.

Conclusion

Despite the fact that the general advice workers in the health profession offer to pregnant women on exercise today is usually to carry on, the long-held convictions that sport might affect fetal growth and bring on abortion or premature labor have not disappeared. Although many women contest the boundaries of what are considered "appropriate" activities and have demonstrated that sport can be continued during pregnancy, many activities are still considered far too dangerous for pregnant women. It is widely believed that a pregnant woman's primary concern ought be for her unborn child, and to this child she must sacrifice all and risk nothing.

It is significant that few of the thirty-one pregnant women included in my study took up or even kept on with what might be considered high-performance sport. The active sanction against sport may have developed in them a sense of themselves as weak, frail, and sedentary especially in a country such as Aotearoa/New Zealand, where "Sport has been [and continues to be] a predominant focus for cultural identity" *(New Zealand Official 1996 Year Book* 1996, 269).

Exclusion from sport as a paradigm of physical engagement with the world is not merely something that happens to pregnant women. Pregnant women who define themselves and are defined by others as in a "condition"—fragile, weak, awkward, and passive—and who receive little encouragement to engage their body in physical activity will more often than not become weak, awkward, and physically timid.

Cole claims that "Numerous feminist critics have argued that women's physicality and participation in sport offer the space for potentially oppositional or transgressive practices and a site for progressive body politics because they challenge the passivity inscribed on 'women's bodies' " (1994, 15). Although it is possible to counter such claims by examining the ways in which sport has been highly commodified in recent years to reinforce existing gender relations (for example, see Johnston 1996 for three possible, nonexclusive readings of female bodybuilders), nevertheless it is possible to construct an argument that sport in colonial and present-day Aotearoa/New Zealand has provided women with "an emancipation of sorts" (Crawford 1987, 166). Engaging in high-performance sport means that women develop strength, stamina, and muscularity, which contest notions of women as physically weak and incapable. Pregnant women are represented popularly as fragile and certainly not suited to the rigors of sport. Their withdrawal from sport has little to do with corporeal "limitations" (although the materiality of the pregnant body ought not be ignored), but rather is discursively produced.

2

Producing Lesbians

Canonical Proprieties

Robin Peace

There are no such things [as lesbians]—attributed to Queen Victoria

Here come the lesbians . . .—Alex Dobkin, song title from "old LP"

What *did you say you were?*—My mother, circa 1968[1]

Stolen Glances

This chapter seeks to vivify debate surrounding the coeval appearance
(debut? de novo?) of geographies and (dissident) sexualities on the same
stage—the urban, intellectual stage—the stage on which intellectualized,
sexualized geographical knowledge is being produced, codified, and rei-
fied. In the theaters of intellectual debate surrounding questions of place
and identity, the pleasures of knowledge about lesbian bodies and the
pleasures of knowledge production by lesbian bodies in the academy continue to be constrained by the paradoxical proprieties of real material
bodies.

Or, to put this another way . . .

This is a circular argument within an embracing pose. The central

---

1. These quotations are not literal but rather are sayings designed to be reminders that
the identity question in relation to the category *lesbian* exists in the vernacular as much as in
the academic text.

focus is the "body" of the lesbian and the question of lesbian identity in the context of the production of geographical knowledge. In this first section on the body and the text, I suggest that lesbian geographies (an epistemological question) and geographies of lesbians (an ontological question) pose quite different problems in relation to the nature of geographical knowledge produced in the academy and to the ways in which such knowledge is deployed. The second pose, extrapolated from the concept of geographies of lesbians, concerns the more specific issue of the visibility of lesbian bodies and the exclusions, inclusions, and politics of lesbian identity in the city. I touch on relationships between visibility, performance, and commodification.[2] I suggest that the ways in which desire (Grosz 1995) forms a controversial but incontrovertible aspect of lesbian identity exposes the lesbian body to interpellation as a consumer-citizen rather than as an improper[3] body in her own (rightful) place. The commodification and exposure of lesbian identity (intricately imbricated with the issue of desire) not only provides greater access to a visible (mappable) identity, but also provides a greater resource from which geographies of lesbians may be produced. In the third and final pose, I reflect on the question of "improper" bodies in geography to examine the concept of abjection and return to the epistemological concept of *lesbian geography.*

This chapter explores not the street-level pleasures of lesbian desire, but the pleasures, paradoxes, and proprieties of academic representations of *lesbian* in the context of *geography*—pleasures of a more cerebral sort, perhaps, but pleasures that are intrinsically tied to questions of material place and identity both within and beyond the academy. I question the paradox of "the lesbian" as an ephemeral subject, the paradox of invisibility for geographical subjects, and the corporeal paradoxes of the improper body of the lesbian geographical subject.

The focus throughout this chapter is on *lesbian* as opposed to *homosex-*

2. *Commodification* in this sense refers not only to the idea of "shopping" in a very everyday sense, but also to the idea that "purchase agreements" in relation to identity operate at the level of the imaginary and the symbolic. I am indebted to a reading of Mary Douglas and Baron Isherwood's *The World of Goods* (first published 1979) for the potential of this argument.

3. *Improper:* "not truly or strictly belonging to the thing under consideration, not in accordance with truth, fact, reason or rule; abnormal; irregular; incorrect; inaccurate; erroneous; wrong" (*Compact Oxford Dictionary* 1991, 825). The arguments surrounding desire and propriety are, unfortunately, beyond the scope of this chapter. I am indebted to Elizabeth Grosz (1995, particularly 173–85) for her contribution to this discussion.

ual male or *queer* geographies, as a gentle resistance to the ongoing—but increasingly subtle—privileging of the male in geography.[4] As Gillian Rose has already claimed, "the academic discipline of geography has historically been dominated by men," and there has been an ongoing "intertwining of masculine subjectivities and academic geographical knowledge" (1993, 1, 137). Steve Pile admits to understanding that "behavioural geography is constituted through an implicit, undisclosed, oppressive and obstructive masculinism" (1995, 19). And, Vera Chouinard and Ali Grant reiterate that "the new 'Project' in radical geography" (the "Project" that recognizes feminism and postmodernism, and redraws Marxist approaches to the discipline) is "in some ways . . . as partial and exclusionary as those that have gone before" (1996, 170). In particular, they comment on the silences surrounding the "living exclusions" that lesbian and disabled women experience in the academy. Arguments about lesbians and geographies of access (such as theirs and my own) refrain from further reification of a masculine subject even if they may never subvert the masculinized epistemologies within which geographical knowledges are lodged. In this argument, my reference to the lesbian and the lesbian body is more metaphorical than literal because I acknowledge that there is no "real" lesbian around whom these arguments could legitimately coalesce—"she who"[5] is, for the strategy of this argument, a fictive universal.[6]

4. That there is an ongoing privileging of the male in geography may be open to dispute, but my visceral sense is that the lacuna that may always be anticipated in the academy is the one that identifies the lesbian body: scratch any geographical framework, and she will be difficult to find.

5. The phrase *she who* resonates from an old LP recording of the American lesbian poets Pat Parker and Judy Grahn reading their work. It recurs to me in the context of this chapter as I (conservatively and unimaginatively) resist the notion of "the lesbian, he."

6. The phrase *stolen glances* in the subtitle of this section refers to the book title from which Steve Pile sourced an ambiguous photograph that he uses to mark the conclusion to his book *The Body and the City* (1996). The photograph, *"The Knight's Move" series 1990*, was taken by Tessa Boffin and appears in a book edited by Tessa Boffin and Jane Fraser. Whereas this photograph and its accompanying caption is the only reference to *lesbian* in Pile's book, I am using observations and reflections (on this photograph and other matters) in my own chapter to encapsulate some of my own "stolen glances" at the issue of lesbians and geography and to acknowledge the partiality of the representation.

The Body and the Text

The insertion of *lesbian* into the (psycho)dynamics of "intellectual space" in a geographical sense is highly problematic. Two of the core pleasures, core identifiers, of the discipline of geography lie in the field and on the map. There are current but unresolved arguments about the empirical bases of geographical knowledge, about the conflation of the map and representation (Kirby 1996; Pickles 1992; Sibley 1995), but there is a persistent sense that group categorization relies on field observation and "mappability." In geographical terms, the grouping of human activities in space enables patterns of distribution to be discerned, studied, and mapped. "Grouping" implies that there are certain attributes, elements, or characteristics that can be held to belong together enough to be subjected to an identifying gaze—to be seen to be real. If the category *lesbian* is somehow invisible in these terms (which is contestable), geographers may need to think of how the project of representation of *lesbian* as a *marked* and *unmarked* identity is to proceed. Lesbian interpretations of and reflections on spatial relations or any appreciation of the implications of spatial relationships to the embodied category *lesbian* may have the heuristic capacity to uncouple, or at least to destabilize, this relationship between the field and the map. It might be useful to reflect on the question of whether the category *lesbian* constitutes an identifiably "spatialized," mappable, "real" identity group or whether, problematically, it belongs somehow in Baudrillard's (1983) category of the simulacrum and is therefore "not real," not mappable, not geographical. Baudrillard claims that "abstraction today is no longer that of the map, the double, the mirror or the concept. . . . The territory no longer precedes the map, nor survives it. . . . it is the map that engenders the territory" (1983, 2). His elaboration here is poignant:

> for it is the difference [between the real and the abstraction] which forms the poetry of the map and the charm of the territory, the magic of the concept and the charm of the real. This representational imaginary, which both culminates in and is engulfed by the cartographer's mad project of a coextensivity between the map and the territory, disappears with simulation—whose operation is nuclear and genetic, and no longer specular and discursive. (1983, 3).

To carry Baudrillard's logic forward is to assert the lesbian as simulation. There is a frisson of danger in failing to resolve the difference between the "real" and the "abstraction" that is not only to do with the failure of a "poetics of [mappable] space"[7], but also (and more unnervingly) to do with failure of *lesbian* to be an identity rather than a simulation. This issue is beyond the scope of my argument, but its salience is cautionary.

Three questions suggest themselves as central to some resolution of identity paradox in terms of this spatial discourse: First, is *lesbian* a category that can be called into being for the purposes of geographical analysis? To what extent is a lesbian a citizen amenable to mapping? Second, if the category *lesbian* exists (and human subjects occupy that category by self or other definition), is that category *placeless*—as Manuel Castells suggested in a 1983 publication that geographers have yet to challenge seriously? Finally, is it space, policy,[8] or identity that is crucial to the marking up[9] of the category *lesbian* for inclusion within the canon or discourse of geography? I return to Castells's argument shortly.

Ultimately, subjectivity and the acknowledgment of the extent to which the notion of the lesbian (subject) is, in herself, a troublesome term in any geographical debate are crucial. There are various grounds on which

7. Bachelard's *The Poetics of Space* can be bent to underwrite this idea succinctly: "For here the cultural past doesn't count. . . . One must be receptive to the image at the moment it appears. . . . To say that the poetic image is independent of causality is to make a rather serious statement" (1969, 1:xiii). To write/produce/identify a poetics of lesbian space may be a way to map this geography.

8. I use the term *policy* frequently in this chapter. Titmuss suggests a broad definition of *policy* that suits the purposes of my use of the term: "the principles that govern action directed towards given ends" (1974, 23). In other words, policies are not necessarily formal, written documents and frameworks, but include protocols, approaches, unwritten codes, and general principles that operate *as if* they were formal, published, explicit frameworks and codes. The role of "implicit" policies in the production and approval of appropriate knowledge is important to my argument.

9. The phrase *marking up* is used here in the sense of labeling commodities with a bar code that indicates both product type and value. My suggestion is that some identifying act is always required to "produce" the lesbian body for the gaze and that increasingly the publication of lesbian identity depends on acts of commodification—whether that be through the entertainment display of a gay parade or through the purchase and display of more individualized "markers"—hair cuts, tattoos, jewelry, magazines, movies, and so on (see also Holliday, chapter 3 in this volume).

the lesbian can be inducted into the canon, but there is also an epistemic question about the need for a radical reconceptualization of ephemeral subjectivity. As a potential "geographical" presence in the concrete, com-modified spaces of the city, the lesbian needs to exist not as something (someone?) that (who) exists in the minds of man (*sic*)—a tagged, stereo-typical bull dagger wielding her whip over the exposed buttocks of the (masculine) street in an ecstasy of gay pride—but a something else.

Questions of sexuality and identity are being rigorously examined elsewhere (see Butler 1990, 1993; Duncan 1996; Frye 1983, 1992; Fuss 1989, 1991; Grosz 1989b, 1994, 1995; Grosz and Probyn 1995; Keith and Pile 1993; Pile 1996; Pile and Thrift 1995; Sibley 1995, for example). Such debates may need to become interdisciplinary commons if the questions "What is a les-bian? Who is she?" are to be acknowledged in geographic discourse.

As a stylistic ornamentation to this argument, I make deliberate use of chiastic phrasing in order to claim the difference between "lesbian geogra-phies" and the "geography of lesbians"[10] in this first section, and between "essential politics" and "political essentials," and "viable sites" and "sites of viability" at subsequent stages. Chiasma are like riddles, in a sense. They drive the imagination to leap the gap between the straightforward and the obscure, between the explicit and the implicit, and so to produce a cross-threaded fascination that highlights conceptual tensions and lacunae.

Lesbian Geographies

At least three interpretations of what is encompassed by the field of lesbian geographies is possible, but in all three cases lesbian subjectivity is central.

10. The epistemic debate about lesbian geography/geography of lesbians has resonance in Aotearoa/New Zealand with a current troubling debate about Māori geography, where there is a specific and potent understanding that this geography is not solely of and about things and people Māori, but is also a claim against the knowledge base of conventional ge-ography. Māori geography instantiates a Māori reading of the landscape in which, say, repre-sentations of *taniwha* hold immediate and palpable spatial significance (Stokes 1987). The capacity of Māori geography to destabilize Pākehā understandings of what geography is may perhaps be tenable only in the unique postcolonial landscapes of Aotearoa/New Zealand, where treaty rights embody the rights of Māori to the *taonga* (treasures) of knowledge. That there are no treaty rights conferring status (or knowledge rights) on queer bodies suggests some of the identity complexity that adheres to any group identity that is founded on desire alone.

The first case can be understood to be about work produced by lesbian geographers about lesbians. It is work that is authored by (a self-identified?)
lesbian and takes the subject of lesbians as its object. Perhaps this work is
also designed for consumption by lesbian audiences, and perhaps it reflects some of the terms of internal debate within some kind of (lesbian)
community. Lesbian geographies could also arguably include work authored by lesbians but is not about anything ostensibly lesbian at all. Recent debates about "standpoint epistemologies," and "situated
knowledges" (Haraway 1988; Harding 1991) would endorse such a position, where it is assumed that the speaking subject reflects her own subjectivity in her work—however obliquely. It could also be argued—and this is
a radical suggestion from outside an essentialist debate about who has the
right to speak for whom (only lesbians may speak about lesbians)—that
lesbian geographies also include the records of reflexive discussions and
debates about ontology and epistemology in geography in which the lesbian is prefigured. Heterosexuals (women or men) or homosexual men or
otherwise nonlesbian discussants who nevertheless identify the category
or the embodiment of *lesbian* might author such debates. In all three of
these positions, *lesbian* preempts geography, and *lesbian* provides the subject for whatever geographical sentence follows. In all of these arenas, the
writing "body" of the lesbian (author) or lesbian-identified author provides the access to the geographies. *Lesbian* is a *marked* identity, a corporeal
presence who marks the text even if she is not yet understood to be a
marker[11] on the landscape.

There are issues of confidentiality in the production of lesbian geography: To what extent do lesbians want to become visible in the academic
text—either to be made over to the object position or to become marked up
as a contentious (exotic and interesting) subject? As Biddy Martin suggests, to separate out the category *lesbian* creates a situation in which "lesbianism loses its potential as a position from which to read against the
grain of narratives of normal life course, and becomes simply the affirma-
tion of something separated out and defined as 'lesbian' " (1993, 275). It
may be that to write the lesbian into the text of space in fact confounds the

11. I draw on a literal as well as an anthropological use of the term *marker*. As Douglas
and Isherwood suggest, "marking draws on the meanings of the hallmarking of gold and sil-
ver and pewter, the signing of unlettered persons of their intentions, the authenticating of
work" (1996, 50).

oppositional identity on which the category depends. It may also go some way to explain the opposition from within lesbian groups themselves to research of any kind, and particularly to research that identifies the places in which lesbians live, work, and read their lives "against the grain" (Adler and Brenner 1992; Johnston and Valentine 1995). Martin's observation reinforces the idea that an argument for a lesbian geography is an argument for a strategic, political inclusion of a marginalized, unstable, and basically invisible identity. Lesbian geography is an issue of "identity politics," and the development of a lesbian geography depends first on a claim against existing policy (a deconstructive move) and only then on "what follows" in terms of an antiessentialist challenge to the idea of lesbian identity.

Political Essentials

In the brief discussion that follows, I draw on the work of Diana Fuss, who in her 1989 book *Essentially Speaking* has done much both to summarize the complex arguments for and against "essential" notions of identity and to locate those arguments within an explicitly political framework. It is a political logic that drives me to suggest that some clear agenda of (and for) lesbian geography within the canon is essential. The politics that drives a lesbian academic to make an emancipatory claim for the inclusion of lesbian geography is premised on a perceived causal link between identity and politics, and therefore must assume the existence of the essential lesbian identity. Fuss suggests, however, that there is a precarious status to identity per se (whether lesbian or whatever other) and that providing any fixed definition for an identity may not solve the problem of the political constitution of that identity. If it could be said, and I believe it could be, that a politics of identity argument will provide the conditions of possibility for lesbian geography, then, as Fuss suggests, it is the politics as much as the identity that needs to be called into question. Fuss states: "A series of unanswered questions pose themselves as central to any current discussions of identity politics. Is politics based on identity, or is identity based on politics?" (1989, 100).

Jacques Rancière puts this in another way, or in fact provides some answer to the questions Fuss poses, when he suggests that in trying to locate universal claims to equality in an idea of citizenship, or of universal human-beingness, we are looking in the wrong direction. "Do we or do we not belong to the category of men or citizens or human beings, and what follows from this? The universality is not enclosed in *citizen* or *human being;* it is involved in the 'what follows,' in its discursive and practical enactment" (1992, 60). In other words, the political does not in fact lie in the identity (of citizen, of lesbian), but in the "what follows."

Essentially Political

What follows in this brief detour of my argument is a challenge to a disciplinary[12] policy that privileges visible, tangible, spatial interactions and excludes whatever eludes the scrutiny of the gaze. There is a policy or set of policies (some explicitly stated on the inside covers of academic journals and some more obscurely held within the heads of book and journal editors) that create the boundaries and definitions of any particular disciplinary knowledge. These policies are subject to contestation and reevaluation through specific emancipatory claims—claims that challenge the existing parameters and exclusions of the discipline. Human geography has been through (and is going through) this process most recently with feminist (see Bondi 1990, 1993; Duncan 1996; McDowell 1991, 1996) and postcolonial (see Anderson 1996; Brah 1996; Chambers and Curti 1996; Hesse 1993) critiques. It went through it earlier under positivist, humanistic, structuralist, and welfarist critiques. It is this process of contestation within the area of policy formation that generates Rancière's concept of the political. A dialogic space of encounter is engendered when emancipatory claims contest policy. Stanley Brunn, former editor of *Annals of the Association of American Geographers* and policymaker for the publications in that journal, points to this argument by omission in this statement: "the voids in the worlds we study and include as part of our discipline would seem to be our concern. . . . There is also a need to explore how our discipline's pasts and presents relate to the emerging and exciting interdisciplinary field of disciplinary history" (1992, 2). He is suggesting that "we" have to fill the void by speaking for the other, by making their concerns "our concern." Lesbians are not specifically alluded to in his long catalogue of what is (a)voided by geography. He makes a proprietorial suggestion that there is a "we" speaking here. This "we" is a category of geographers who have

12. I am referring here to the policies of academic *disciplines,* with all the rich connotations of that word for control, limitation, containment, and propriety.

some shared understandings about what it is that "our" discipline studies. These geographers have an identity from which to make claims about the void. It might seem, on the basis of Brunn's logic, that only those already within the canon can participate in emancipatory claims.

To challenge such a policy would require "we" geographers to think about the idea that lesbians are not avoided innocently; to think about what is at stake in demands for confidentiality on the part of potential subjects; to think of ways that ephemeral or unmarked categories might be represented; and finally to think about the implications of failing to engage with lesbian geography as one of "our [disciplinary] concerns." What will follow from an encounter, in this political space of self-interrogation, between our policy as geographers and the claim for the emancipation of lesbian space may be a refashioning of discursive space in order to provide a proper place in geography for "improper" bodies and places.

Who is most likely to make an emancipatory claim for lesbian geography? And who has most to lose by appearing to claim, as if they knew what they were talking about, on behalf of this community? Brunn does not suggest that this question is political, but it is political in the sense that what is published in geographical journals and academic texts (and therefore to a large extent what is defined as "geography") is subject to policy. The policy is created, laid down, proscribed by the editorial boards of journals and does indeed bound what can be considered as "legitimate" foci for geography. To follow Rancière's argument, emancipatory claims can be made only on the basis of an identity—but this is not a simple thing. As he suggests, "the logic of political subjectivization, of emancipation, is a heterology, a logic of the other. . . . First it is never the simple assertion of an identity; it is always, at the same time, the denial of an identity given by an other, given by the ruling order of policy. Policy is about 'right' names, names that pin people down to their place and work" (1992, 62).

The question, to which I return in the penultimate section of this chapter, is indeed that of "right names." Geography does appear to depend on a notion or set of notions that people have a place (a "right" place) in relation to their environment and that this place is related to some notion or set of notions about identity and about the rightness and propriety embodied in certain identity categories and in the places they occupy.

Deferential Policies

One way, perhaps, to bring the category *lesbian* out is to defer to it.[13] Such deference can be accomplished through a deconstructive critique of the grounds on which geographers construct the particular notions of space with which they work and that are so central to the discipline. To defer to it thus is to create the political space for lesbian geography by debating the grounds on which this identity/nonidentity has hitherto been excluded from the canon. To defer to it is also to defer the debate about what that identity might or might not entail and therefore to defer the possibility of lesbian geographies. As Butler suggests, "this is not to say that I will not appear at political occasions under the sign of lesbian, but that I would like to have it permanently unclear what precisely that sign signifies" (1993, 308). Such a proposition forbids closure—leaves the space open for the recuperation and renegotiation of desire as a geographical subject. Agreement with such a proposition also encourages me to acknowledge that there is no clear zone for the pleasures of lesbian geography, yet perhaps there are pleasures to be had, as a lesbian if nothing else, in the formation of geographies of lesbians. With an eye to the city as a site for the presentation of the lesbian body, I address the issue of lesbian geographies in the next section.

Geographies of Lesbians

Following a "standard rule" of English language formation, the subject of the title phrase is *geographies*. The lesbian, were she to figure, would figure as the object; the lesbian would be transfixed (like any other research object) and represented in a range of geographical discourses as that which (or she who) had been studied. This should be the accessible stuff of a "geographical" approach, and it would not be unreasonable to expect that there would be as much (if not more, why not?) written about lesbians in

13. This is a classic Derridean pose. Deference is a two-edged instrument: we defer to that which is superior or to that which we acknowledge requires a place, but we also defer in the sense of suspending judgements. We defer both in the sense of submission and postponement, and express deference in yet a third sense—of compliance and respect.

the geographical canon as there is about gypsies or blacks or gays. As a geographer, I could reasonably expect to find research about lesbian migration, lesbian employment, lesbian election patterns, lesbian economies, lesbian health, lesbian housing and so on ad nauseam/infinitum (could I not?). However, lesbian identity is paradoxical and problematic, opaque and indecipherable. It marks an "absence of presence"—something ephemeral—an unmarked category inaccessible to representation in "good" geographies that seek to identify the spatial relationships between people and their environments or, more courageously, that seek to problematize issues of people and place. Not only do geographies of lesbians not put in an appearance in the so-called conventional geographies—in the core descriptive texts (the mainstream theater) about the subject (such as Gregory, Martin, and Smith 1994; Rogers, Viles, and Goudie 1992; or R. Johnston 1991), but neither do they put in much of an appearance in the fringe productions (but see Bell et al. 1994; Bell and Valentine 1995b; Valentine 1992, 1993a, 1993b), where the geographical object is more likely to be the masculinized queer object—the gay male. There is no reason why the canon is not as saturated with lesbiana as it is with issues of ethnicity, gender, or, particularly, class.[14] But there must be a reason, a rationale, for a politics of exclusion that is so unremarked, so unmarkable. In the next section of this chapter, I tease out some thoughts about this exclusionary politics. I attempt to essay the strength of it and to find one seam at least, along which an epistemological rupture might be foreshadowed.

Exclusionary Politics—Ephemeral Subjects

Valentine has suggested that lesbians "construct multiple sexual identities in different time-space frameworks" (1993b, 237). The challenge for geography is how to cope with a subject that has no fixed, natural, assignable, mappable essence. Considering the question as a political one, in the first instance, may serve to open a space for debate about the conceptual and methodological pleasures and problems that geographies of lesbians appear to pose.

If the category *lesbian* is unstable and historically and culturally spe-

14. I suggest *class* in particular because it is the representation of externalized embodiment—embodiment that is commonly understood to be wholly socially constructed rather than partially (or fully) the product of genes.

cific, then there is no condition under which a lesbian universal can be instantiated unproblematically in geographical or any other discourse. For the few geographers who have attempted to work with this category, the invisible/visible paradox creates problems of representation. In attempting to deal with this paradox, some geographic researchers have concluded that lesbians are *placeless*—that is, they or their actions and behaviors do not produce "mappable" patterns of distribution. Others have resolved the problem by focusing on places that lesbians do inhabit, thereby producing a kind of proxemics where the feeling for space between people is manifest in visible cultural artifacts such as buildings and venues.

Both of these approaches to geographies of lesbians suggest the possibility that the refusal to acknowledge geographies of lesbians is a political question that the discipline of geography, with its insistence on the existence of visible categories of subjects, needs to engage. The question to be considered then is, How and in what ways might the discipline of human geography come to terms with ephemeral (contingently visible) or liminal (at the threshold of the visible) identity as a legitimate object/subject of study?

The groundbreaking (but already superseded?) work of Manuel Castells on homosexual geographies is worth returning to at this point. Castells's own background in urban ecology studies produces his focus on "place" and "urban hierarchy," where "the city is posited as a gathering at a higher level of individuals or groups" (1977, 102), and it is within this urban context that Castells suggests that lesbians are "placeless." He appears to be suggesting that lesbians both within their own community and in their relations with the wider community are not part of "an empirically mappable type of territorial collectivity" (102).

Castells is identifying lesbians as not the same as homosexual males in that lesbians' otherness may produce something different from the "straightforward," conspicuous place occupancy of gay males. He identifies this difference in attitudes to space and territoriality. In identifying a difference between gays and lesbians in order to justify his exclusion of the lesbian from his discussion, he resorts to a representation of difference between male/female. By using this dichotomy as an unproblematic departure point, he is able to confidently claim that "there is a major difference between men and women in their relationship to space. Men have sought to dominate, and one expression of this domination is spatial. . . . Women have rarely had these territorial aspirations" (1983, 140).

There are at least five sweeping generalizations here: that the category *lesbian* conflates with the category *woman;* that women (as a category that includes lesbians?) have no expressions of territoriality in their repertoires; that men have actively sought to dominate space; and that in so doing they are responding to some innate territorial imperative; and, finally, that gay men are the same as (heterosexual) men.

On the basis of incorporating but not challenging these assumptions, Castells asserts that San Francisco is the world's gay capital; that gays in San Francisco have "uniquely succeeded in building up a powerful . . . independent community at spatial, economic, cultural and political levels" (1983, 138); and that this representation of community has the deeper significance of expressing the "emergence of a social movement and its transformation into a political force through the spatial organization of a self-defined cultural community" (1983, 138). In this identification of a bounded community, he accords San Francisco's gay male community the conditions of possibility for their existence within the canon: they become a visible, identifiable (albeit contestable) community upon which the geographic gaze, hungry for new and exotic landscapes, may fall.

Nowhere in his analysis does Castells question assumptions of identity. And in that analysis, the lesbian is denied—is "placeless" and "tends not to acquire a geographical basis for their political organisation" (1983, 138). In his earlier work, Castells argues:

> this does not mean that the concentration of certain social characteristics in a given space has no effect and that there cannot be any link between a certain ecological site and cultural specificity . . . but for such effects to be manifested, there must first of all be the social production of a certain cultural autonomy, and this production depends on the place occupied in the relations of production, and the institutional system and the system of social stratification. (1977, 108)

Given his Marxist perspectives, Castells may have found it difficult to place lesbians because they appeared to be outside conventional relations of production (and I return to this point later) and were placeless in that sense. What he is specific about, however, is that his research is about the relationship between sociocultural revolt and the city. In this focus, he circumscribes his study to a particular set of representations in space—namely, local body / voter / activist political representations. Perhaps, in the early 1980s, gay male political activity was indeed most evident in San Francisco's space. However, by narrowing his focus in this way, Castells fails to consider that maybe something more is going on in the positioning of lesbians in the political than their "placelessness." In setting up the notion of the innate, possibly biological, territorial imperative, he (perhaps unwittingly?) laid the ground for some interesting territorial maneuvers on the part of gay male geographers who were quick to exploit and elaborate the notion of gay occupancy of space (but see Tamar Rothenberg's [1995] riposte to Castells in which she specifically concentrates on the evolution of lesbian "territory" in New York).

Much of the geography that has been produced under the flag of "gay geographies" has been based on spatial location models of gay male occupancy of space. Such work has an ecological or ethnographic emphasis in which either the spatial patterns of social artifacts are emphasized or there has been an attempt to provide "an empathetic understanding of a particular environment from the perspective of the subjects themselves" (Jackson and Smith 1984, 175). In such studies, the subject is constructed as "other" in order to be made an object of the gaze. Gay identity was assumed to be unproblematic in as much as the artifacts attached to that identity— namely, real estate (Knopp 1990a, 1990b) or voter participation in local body politics (Moos 1989) or the sites of Mardi Gras (Seebohm 1992)— could be mapped. Perhaps it is not possible to cartographically interpellate lesbians?

Some (mostly lesbian) narrators have made attempts to install some notion of geographies of lesbians within the existing canon. More often than not, such efforts have been confined to the bedroom rather than to the boardroom. Citations in the few published articles invariably list research that is not yet published (master's research, dissertations, unpublished doctoral work, unpublished conference papers; see Beyer 1992; Peace n.d., forthcoming), which is, if you like, the "bedroom" work. However, there *is* some "boardroom" geography of lesbians in the published canon.

Visible Inclusions

In each case of published material (see Adler and Brenner 1992; Johnston and Valentine 1995; Munt 1995; Rothenberg 1995; Valentine 1992, 1993a, 1993b, 1996; Winchester and White 1988), the work has involved the identification of some visible artifacts, which could be said to stand as signifiers of a lesbian community, and the subsequent location of these artifacts in space—urban housing, the home, the streets, urban neighborhoods, loci of contact, multiple identities for multiplicities of spaces and entertainment centers. None of these papers fully engage with the problematic nature of *lesbian* as an identity category per se or with the more problematic, epistemic concept of lesbian geography.

In the next section, I rove over a range of suggestive possibilities to do with visibility, performativity, and commodification of lesbian geographic subjects, while being (parenthetically, at least) conscious of the "policy question" about what constitutes geography as a subject discipline. Always pushing at the margins is the dual premise that human geography is preoccupied with the question of people and their relationship to the environment and with the accumulation of data that is amenable to "mapping." And geography is also preoccupied with the "real," despite the recent postmodern identification of the ubiquity and utility of spatial metaphors. Sally Munt, on the other hand, suggests that lesbian identity and embodiment are constructed in the mobilization of (specifically) urban space: "Lesbian identity is constructed in the temporal and linguistic mobilisation of space, and as we move *through* space we imprint utopian and dystopian moments upon urban life. Our bodies are vital signs of this temporality and intersubjective location" (1995, 125). The body is the crux of the matter: Is there or is there not a "lesbian body"? Is there or is there not an absence of lesbian (body) presence in the geographical texts of the world? Is there or is there not a visible, mappable body of (lesbian) bodies than can be said/seen to occupy the stage, to steal the scene, to be embodied place holders with a stake in geographical representation? Is the "lesbian body" that geographers already glance at somehow fetishized by consumption and desire, to be "marked up" and understood to be only one kind of (profligate, young, urban) body? And is this a "real" body or a body whose identity is mobilized only in specific time/space moments?

Tagging Consumption as the Signifier: The Paradox of Invisible Subjects

In this (somewhat playful) subheading, I suggest that consumption, along with the visibility of consumable items, is as much a key signifier of the "invisible" lesbian as it is of "invisible" class. I argue that geographies of lesbians are necessarily intensified processes of *cultural tagging*[15] in which access to the geography of lesbians is premised on "visibility factors"—on a "marking up" of the lesbian body (see Bell and Valentine 1995d). I suggest that the intensification of identity through the commodification of pleasure and desire may become a means by which the ephemeral category can be signified. As Douglas and Isherwood suggest,

> Treat the goods then as markers, the visible bit of the iceberg which is the whole social process. Goods are used for marking in the sense of classifying categories . . . There may be private marking, but here we refer to public use. Goods are endowed with value by the agreement of fellow consumers. They come together to grade events, upholding old judgements or reversing them. Each person is a source of judgements and a subject of judgements; each individual is in the classification scheme whose discriminations [s]he is helping to establish. (1996, 51)

By this interpretation, two identifiers come into play: one is the ephemera of things in themselves, and the other is the group consensus on the value of those things. The "things" used to identify the lesbian—the body marking, the parade costumes, the style of clothing, the designated venues—all work as markers. The value of these things may either be accorded within the interior dialogues of particular groupings and subgroupings within the (lesbian) "community" or be applied from outside in either negative or positive terms. These "markups" of the lesbian body occur in overtly politicized, public space. Ironically, it is the "immaterial thing" of lesbianism—same-sex desire—that is most clearly understood to "identify" the lesbian, and this unmarked ephemera of the lesbian body occurs in the covertly politicized, private space—or does it? The consumption of the body—the highly sexualized "devouring desire"—is both *the* most private and *the* most identifying lesbian act. "Doing it" *is* what marks the body. Here is the paradox of the queer body that makes for difficult geographies, and here the constraints of the feminine and the constraints of

15. I invent the term *cultural tagging* to cover a range of social practices designed to highlight the identity of an otherwise ambiguous body. For example, the wearing of "labrys" jewelry or tattoos, "dykey" haircuts, leathers, or butch insignia may be seen to signify a "lesbian body" (though all of these markers are themselves malleable, impermanent, subject to mimicry), just as *moko* (traditional Māori facial tattooing) would be understood to signify a "Māori body" in Aotearoa/New Zealand, even if the body was visibly "white."

age, class, and background paradoxically mark the lesbian body differently from the body of the gay male. David Bell's résumé of gay urban fragments (chapter 4 in this volume) inadvertently spells out this paradox. In identifying the public toilet/cottage, the disco, the gay bar, the urban wastelands, and the transit station as the public sites of private pleasures, Bell identifies the spaces for the performance of gay male sexual rituals. These sites are not necessarily or even likely to be the sites of lesbian sexual acts, even if they may sometimes be the sites of more discreet lesbian performativity. It may not be unknown for two (New Zealand)[16] women to have a sexual encounter in a public toilet, but it is unlikely that public toilets (in New Zealand) are understood to be potential sites of sexual liaison between women. It is even unlikely that many lesbians use toilet sites as a place to meet other lesbians. Bars and disco venues, however, are used as meeting places, but factors of age and class militate against their ubiquity. It could be argued, therefore, that one of the constraints on the pleasure of producing geographies of lesbians is the misrecognition of public and private lesbian places and spaces.

In the next section, I use the third chiastic frame—viable sites or sites of viability—to examine the specificity of the "temporal and linguistic mobilisation of space" (Munt 1995, 125) in terms of the "marked up" lesbian body in the city. On the one hand, I suggest that the geographically viable lesbian body is constructed in spaces of consumption and (material) desire. The sites at which or on which a lesbian body can be (visibly) located depend on access to (city) sites of consumption. On the other hand, and in the involuted logic of the chiasmas, I suggest that access to such sites depends on particularities of comportment and propriety not just in the heteronormative sphere but within the more private protocols of lesbian normativity. Cities and the visibility entailed in "being lesbian" in the public spaces of the city are tied to particular kinds of consumption and desire.

Viable Sites

For the purpose of this next piece of my argument, still frangible, still tentative, I assume that cities (Western, capitalist cities) are sites through which the lesbian body moves and within which lesbians may have access

16. It is important to remember that this view is an antipodean view. It may be that lesbian mores "upstairs" in the Northern Hemisphere are quite different.

to a "made-visible" lesbian identity. Within these cities, also, I assume that lesbians have access to specific lesbian pleasures—pleasures for the lesbian body as consumer citizen, priced and paid for. The sites at which public transactions of lesbian identity take place are places of purchase (lesbians kissing in the supermarket?). It is not the purpose of the argument in this chapter to do more than skirt around this complex and provocative claim. The "ready-made" understandings are that lesbians (and others) can buy their way into designated places in which their identity either may be or is proclaimed: lesbian discos, clubs, saunas, restaurants, cafés, bookshops, bed and breakfast houses, motels, sports clubs. By "being there," they can "be." In a similar, but perhaps more nuanced way, specific body markers such as a shaved head, a labrys tattoo, or a leather jacket can mark the space of the individual body. In these sites, it is viable to be a visible lesbian body, and it is the space that is mobilized through time and discourse to produce the signified (see also Holliday, chapter 3 in this volume).

When Steve Pile writes a book entitled *The Body in the City*, he is apparently not referring to a lesbian body. The body of the lesbian (a lesbian?) is not altogether absent from his book; a close reading of the introductory pages finds the following acknowledgment: " '*The Knight's Move*' series *1990* by Tessa Boffin, in Tessa Boffin and Jean Fraser (eds.), *Stolen Glances: Lesbians Take Photographs,* Pandora Press" (1996, x). There is no further reference to any specific lesbian body—although the photograph that is acknowledged duly appears on page 239 as the graphic piece for the book's conclusion. It is a photograph of a young woman? a dyke? a queer boy? a performance? Joan? dressed in a suit of armor, hand on sword hilt, visored helmet under the left arm—a classic pose (of a knight errant?)—a symbol for a "relationship between meaning, identity and power" (Pile 1996, 245). The lesbian signifier in the photograph is marked out by dress, by hair style, by comportment, and by the well-circulated symbolism of Joan of Arc (the first butch killer dyke ever?), and is posed before the camera to be devoured by the audience of voyeurs who will buy and read the book in which she is displayed. But there is an absent presence of the lesbian as person in the book. It is precisely this absent presence of the lesbian body that is the crux of this matter. A marked and unremarked and remarkable signifier (of what?) appears and disappears and reappears between the columns, between the sheets, between all the representable (but sometimes unmentionable—*pace* Murray 1995) spaces of public and private urban life and steals a glance or steals a persona for display.

The commodification of the extraordinary identity of the lesbian—the culturally tagged body, the visible stereotype (the bull dyke in the whipping parade at the HERO celebrations?)—overpowers the representations of her own other: the public health nurse (in her "sweet blue" frock) or the retired bus driver (with her "sweet white" hair). Certainly, not all transactions of pleasure are commodified, not all are transacted in city spaces, and not all are transacted by "the young." Certainly, there are pleasures to be had that cannot be bought and many pleasures that may be accessed elsewhere than the city. If only as an argument of population density, however, it would be fair to suggest that city sites are more notoriously used in the pursuit of pleasure than more bucolic places. Or, to put it a different way, it is in urban areas that "appropriately public" twentieth-century citizens of the Western industrialized metropolis can comport themselves most easily in the pursuit of pleasures—in finding/buying their hearts' desires. Not only does the city offer a proliferation of sites for the commodification of these material and corporeal desires; it also offers these pleasures to those who have access to them. Access implies both mobility and wealth—the ability to move around in the pursuit of pleasure and the wealth to facilitate both the vivacity to pursue and the capacity to transact when the pursuit is culminated. The processes of consumption, therefore—whether they be in body marking, in public recreation in demarcated lesbian space, or in the performance of stereotypical "dressed identities" and participation in identity parades of various kinds (ironically either those of the justice system, where the lesbian is paraded for the purpose of identifying a lesbian-related crime, or those of the pleasure system, where the lesbian body is displayed in so-called pride parades)—ensure the visibility of the desiring/desireable dyke.

There is a question here to which I cannot do justice in the context of this chapter: Does the production of the public dyke reflect appropriate patterns of consumption that sustain an image of (albeit dissident) propriety? Or are these abject bodies, inappropriately dressed for corporeal citizenship in an urbanized, twentieth-century life? And is it only the "extraordinary" lesbian (the bull dyke, the diesel dyke, the hyperfem) who transacts this commodified identity? If you are an "old" lesbian or a "foreign" lesbian or a "new" lesbian, if you have not been to a "lesbian space" in years, and if you do not conform to whatever current image makes you visible as a lesbian, it is possible that you are not seen. In the liminal space between the transgressive abject and the corporeal propriety to which the lesbian body has access, how then do you become?

Corporeal Paradoxes—Improper Bodies

The city is the site of complex and intensified relationships between strangers.[17] And it is for the interactions between strangers that the commodified display of the lesbian body is so crucial. In a culture that abjures rather than invites intercourse with strangers, the connection between strangers for the transaction of intimate pleasures is highly problematic. Harman suggests that "In order to recognise what the unknown could be, the *known* must first be formulated" (1987, 108, emphasis in the original). The visible cues and clues—the pay and display aspects of publicly sexualized identities—allow for identification and subsequent connection. Sexualized "strangeness" depends implicitly on the powerful parameters of "normative knowing." In the next section, I pursue the thought that "the strange" engenders abjection, and abjection is eschewed wherever possible (Kristeva 1982, 1991). I suggest, in other words, that the most powerful constraint against the production of lesbian geography / geographies of lesbians lies in the capacity of this category of bodies to be misrecognized as the abject corporeal.

Sites of Viability

The paradoxical constraint on the production and consumption of the lesbian body is difficult to articulate, but it rests somewhere in the connection between citizenship, consumption, corporeal propriety, and abjection, and it is to this paradox I now turn. I have used the concept of viability with almost cruel intent in this subheading to return my imagination to the "final stigma" of the lesbian body in a heteronormative world. To be *viable*, according to *The Concise Oxford Dictionary*, is "to be capable of maintaining life; able to live or exist in a particular climate . . . ; able to germinate"

17. Lesley Harman's *The Modern Stranger* (1987) inadvertently provided me with this thought. His book takes for granted an urban basis for the configurations of *stranger* and *familiar*.

(1964, 1449). There are no "legitimate," no "proper" places for the maintenance or germination of lesbian life, just as there are no "proper" (reproductive) avenues for the perpetuation of lesbians.[18] In an oblique way, such
a concept of viability ties into ideas of citizenship. As Carol Pateman (1988)
has so cogently argued, in order to belong (contractually) as a citizen, it is
best if the body is male. In very broad, generic terms, the female body is not
viable as a citizen's body, and the lesbian body—as the perverse shadow, as
the simulacra of the feminine?—even less so.

The category *lesbian* provides access (in Iris Young's [1990c] terms at
least) to the possibility of abjection—both in terms of a self-identified abject
and as the abject "other" of the self-identified heterosexual body. The lesbian body is indeed abject in a number of ways in the context of discourses
of citizenship. In most cases, the lesbian body is not recognized in law
other than pejoratively (but note the exception posed by Dutch law). As a
de facto rather than a de jure body, it has the abject potential of being on the
outside of the law's skin—of being the "other" of the law. The lesbian body
is, arguably, both an ephemeral and a liminal body rather than an incontro-
vertibly material body. The lesbian body is subject to the same range of economic constraints to which the body of woman is subject but has less
capacity as a consumer than the heterosexual or homosexual male body.
The lesbian body can be construed, in Douglas's (1966) classic phrase, as
"matter out of place," as an improper body.

Being abject is, arguably, a constructed but necessary (essential?) state
of being for the lesbian body, as a body that is antithetical to "becoming"
corporeality—in other words, to "appropriate" participation as a public
citizen. But wait, who says that the lesbian body is "unbecoming"? Who
argues the case for "becoming corporeality" as an antilesbian act? The
paronomasia of *becoming* as a play on the philosophical sense of "becoming
a being" and the more colloquial sense of something "looking well on" a
person—as in "Does this dress *become* you?"—serves my argument at this
point. One way *becoming* as in "having a being" can be understood in the
contemporary West is as "having a being who is able to consume": not only
one who is able to consume but one who consumes appropriately, one who

18. These comments are not intended to inflame the debates around surrogacy, lesbian
adoption, lesbian parenting, lesbian marriage, and so on, but rather to acknowledge the extent to which societal norms are still quite fixed to biological understandings of reproduction
and identity.

has the capacity to have all the "right" accoutrements, all the "right" signifiers, and who is consequently "becoming" in the other more colloquial but
also more material sense. In "the final test: culture should fit, not like a
glove, but like a skin. The fake could be bought, but true culture . . . [has] to
grow naturally" (Douglas and Isherwood 1996, 53). Those whom culture
fits as a skin know their place.

The idea of "becoming corporeal" may be read in another, Althusser-
ian way in terms of what is recognized or misrecognized (Easthope and
McGowan 1992) as a subject (or citizen). The citizen carries both a de jure
and a de facto status, and it is around this duality that misrecognition of
the corporeal is possible. The subject who is interpellated—who is hailed
in the street by the billboard, the neon sign, the shopfront window, or the
vendor of wares of any kind—is the consumer. S/he who appears to have
the capacity to consume can equally take on the appearance of the citizen.
The consumer is the citizen-subject of the city par excellence. (And
whether this interpellation occurs through Althusser's mechanisms of ideology and state apparatus is a moot point that need not be pursued here.)
The acceptance of the embodied citizen—the citizen who has a sexualized,
racialized physical presence (as opposed to the abstract presence of mind
of the citizen as voter)—depends on a corporeal becoming, a becoming in
which the body of the citizen accords with a set of guidelines of containment and appropriateness.

Only some bodies may become corporeal citizens—those whose comportment "looks well on" on them. This means that in any city, in any space
in which the citizen pursues pleasure, there will be various categories of
"beings" who do not have a becoming corporeality. Such "unbecoming-
ness" is tied to a range of bodies whose claim on citizenship is tenuous for
a range of (intensified, mainly sociopolitical/cultural) reasons; they may
be bodies that are "inappropriately" feminized, darkened, aged, queered,
or otherwise marginalized. For the purpose of this argument, I suggest that
such bodies can be understood as abject bodies in that they transgress
boundaries of dress in both literal and material senses. Their transgressive
identities are not becoming in the public sphere, where propriety is regu-
lated by formal and informal codes of access. More importantly, the
"proper" body of the citizen is understood as part of a complex, historicist
discourse of Western thought based on chains of signification in which a/-
a dichotomous categories are paramount and where these binary categories provide the conditions of possibility for the "other." The hegemonic

terms of the masculine, the white, the Anglo-European, the young, and the straight provide the idealized comportment of becoming.

This argument pushes at the "logic" of abjection—to find the point (the retch?) at which an ephemeral, liminal lesbian can be acknowledged to inhabit the spaces of the city with no less authority than the gypsy (see Sibley 1995) or the feminist (see Rose 1993) or the black body (see Jackson 1987) or the homosexual male body (see Bell and Binnie, chapters 4 and 5 in this volume).

These unsettled thoughts have no resolution in this text. Questions remain. Is the lesbian body an example of a transgressive, abject body whose corporeality destabilizes notions of access and pleasures? Is it possible to be a citizen if you do not consume the images and become the image of a consumer? I suggest that the lesbian body is ambivalent—sometimes understood as a citizen (the desexed, invisibly corporeal lesbian) and sometimes not (the sexualized, excluded abject corporeal). But, equally, sometimes citizenship accrues to the becoming, highly sexualized lesbian (who passes for straight?) in contemporary chic, and sometimes the abjection accrues to the lesbian who hopes that the closet will protect her citizenship but whose comportment lacks propriety in either a lesbian or a straight citizen worldview. I also suggest that these liminalities in lesbian identity produce a paradoxically spatialized (Rose 1993) embodiment under the myopic gaze of the sexed body (Grosz 1994). To divorce the lesbian body from desire is to divorce from identity, and there is a tricky question about whether sexuality is a necessary currency through which a body, identified as abject, must purchase corporeal propriety or citizenship or both.

In much of the existing thinking about queer consumption and citizenship, the category *lesbian* is variously and arguably strategically conflated with either *woman* or *homosexual*. In either maneuver, she is silenced in the process. So what to do with a silenced, potentially abject, ephemeral subject? What capacity does a disciplined account of people and their relationships to place have to hold onto or represent the ambiguous geographies of the lesbian body?

Conclusion: Ephemeral Streams—
Analogy from the Physical Margins

My own sense is that much of the postmodern challenge to the idea of the unified subject opens the gaps and spaces for this representation and for establishing the conditions of possibility for lesbian geography to exist. One possibility could be produced through the metaphor of liminality, of threshold. The limen—the doorframe, the threshold—becomes the point from which identity is interpellated. In this particular context, for this purpose, "the" lesbian will be called into being: made visible. This is the context in which the researcher contacts that group who, through self-definition, will concede to the research process. For this strategy to produce "good" geography, concessions to the "proper" names of places—streets, towns, and cities—need to be made, which confines geographies of lesbians to the study of those who have "come out." It also allows the lesbian subject(s) a political participation in the production of knowledge about herself/themselves. Valentine (1993a) alludes to this participation in her discussion of the multiple sexual identities that the lesbians she studied worked hard to maintain. If one chose to step through (not outside) the threshold and be lesbian, then that lesbian identity could be partially apparent. Bars, dance venues, picnics, protest banners then become sites at which lesbian identity can be seen to appear. Inasmuch as the *site* is identified as one at which those people who call themselves lesbian at that particular moment in time make their appearance, then lesbian has a spatial location.

As a marked category, the urban lesbian consumer may appear as a geographical signifier open to inclusion in the geographical canon. But I also suggest that liminality—the occupation of a borderland—militates against the interpellation of the lesbian body outside of such urban pleasure zones. Liminal space—the space in which the identity *lesbian* needs to be neither conceded nor denied—is not amenable to mapping. In the occupancy of places such as home or the countryside or even a worksite in which a lesbian might choose to remain closeted, the lesbian may exist as an unmarked category (see also Holliday in this volume). As such, I would argue, she is beyond any geographical purview and occupies an identity position that eludes placement in a geographical sense. No extent of inclusionary politics can call this liminal identity into the canon of the map.

Many lesbian sites (and aspects of lesbian identity) are, however, very temporary. The problem this temporariness poses for geographers—at least in the present discourse of human geography—is that sites that are ephemeral are rarely acknowledged to be constitutive of space. An emphasis on the synchronic predetermines a privileging of the permanent.

Ironically, physical geography offers a useful analogy: the ephemeral stream in arid zones. These streams exist only as traces on the landscape that, under exceptional circumstances such as when it rains in desert areas, become constituted by the water that then streams through them. Geomorphologists, hydrologists, physical geographers defer to the trace and map not the stream but the place where the stream might otherwise flow if a rainstorm were to call it into being. In other words, it is the trace on the landscape rather than the embodiment of the stream with water (the substance we usually understand to constitute a stream) that constitutes the identity of this particular landscape feature. What the ephemerality of the desert stream produces is a shift in our understanding of what a stream is.

Perhaps, as Butler suggests, every interpellation of *lesbian* leads to a shift in understanding:

> To claim that this is what I *am* is to suggest a provisional totalization of this "I." But if the I can so determine itself, then that which it excludes in order to make that determination remains constitutive of the determination itself . . . for it is always unclear what is meant by invoking the lesbian-signifier, since its signification is always to some degree out of one's control, but also because its *specificity* can only be demarcated by exclusions that return to disrupt its claim to coherence. What, if anything, can lesbians be said to share? And who will decide this question and in the name of whom? . . . before, you did not know whether I "am," but now you do not know what that means, which is to say that the copula is empty, that it cannot be substituted for with a set of descriptions. (1993, 309)

The possibility of re-visioned geographical readings of the body in the city—a bringing together of the concrete columns and the warm flesh within a look, a lens, an abstract, a thought-provoking perspective that has the capacity to acknowledge and to see the ways in which stone and flesh, flesh and stone are mutually constitutive—is exciting and is perhaps already begun.

3

(Dis)Comforting Identities

Ruth Holliday

In this chapter, I examine material from video diaries undertaken by a number of people in "queer communities." I am interested in the ways in which identities are performed in different times and spaces—which I will call work, rest, and play—and also how these performances become mediated by academic, political, and "subcultural" discourses of sexuality. I aim to explore the similarities and differences in respondents' accounts and want to chart their *experiences* of identity. In so doing, I hope to illustrate some key aspects of theoretical debates around identity while also considering how far people's experiences of their own identities mirror the fractured selves currently described by academics (for example, Hall 1996) or the theoretical insights of notions of performativity in relation to identity (Butler 1990): Are identities outside the academy experienced as more fixed and less complex than these writings suggest? I would also like to examine how far academic discourses filter into and inform political discourses and what their relevance might be to "vernacular" or "lived" or "subcultural" constructions of the self. In my analysis, then, there are three levels to theorize: the *academic*, and by this I really mean queer theory in this context; the *political*, usually conceived of as lesbian, gay, bisexual, and transgender politics; and the *everyday*, which I call the subcultural (I define these terms in more detail later).

The support of the Economic and Social Research Council (ESRC) is gratefully acknowledged, award number R000236657. I would also like to thank David Bell, Jon Binnie, Azzedine Haddour, Harriette Marshall, Rolland Munro, John O'Neill, and Graham Thompson for reading and commenting on earlier drafts of this chapter.

55

Performing Identities for the Camera

My research has involved giving respondents camcorders and asking them to make video diaries. In the brief for these diaries, respondents were asked to demonstrate (visually) and talk about the ways in which they managed or presented their identities in different settings in their everyday lives. The participants were asked to dress in the clothes they would wear in each situation, describing them in detail and explaining why they thought these self-presentation strategies were appropriate. This technique was designed to make sure that participants were as explicit as possible about the presentation of their identities in different spaces—at work, rest, and play. I then developed theoretical themes as they arose from the data, according to the significance that respondents afforded them and the frequency with which issues arose across all of the respondents' accounts.

I would like to stress the importance of the video diaries in capturing the performativities of identity in ways that are qualitatively different from other sociological research methods. In one sense, the self-representation is more "complete" than in the audiotaped interview, which provides only aural data. The visual dimension of the construction and display of identity is obviously more easily gleaned through this method. In many ways, video diaries have a common currency, largely owing to their recent extended television coverage (in the United Kingdom at least), which makes them a familiar form to respondents. In theory (if not necessarily in practice), video diaries afford respondents more potential than other methods for a greater degree of reflexivity: the diarists in this study could watch, re-record, and edit their diaries before submission, and they had at least one month in which to create their diaries. Regardless of the "accuracy" or "realism" of the diaries, then, they do at least afford the potential for the respondents to represent themselves more fully, unlike other more traditional research methods. For example, Gill[1] says about the process, "Why am I telling you all these things about myself? Well, I think that if you asked me, I'd tell you, but you're going to tell other people; um, because I think that it's important and I think I've got things to say. . . . The least favorite bit of my body is this little bit in here, because I've got a fat bit there, and a front-on picture of my belly, although I let a bit of that be shown ear-

---

1. The names of the diarists have been changed for this chapter.

lier and viewed that to see if I was going to let it stay in." This implies that, in some senses, for her at least, making a video diary can be an empowering process.

I would now like to discuss briefly the location of this chapter with respect to other writings in the field and the particular approach I adopt. Because of the nature of the video diaries and the importance of identity presentations, it is important that I at least gesture toward the relevant literature around consumption, fashion, and dress.

Fashioning the Self

A huge volume of literature is developing around consumption and its meaning, especially focused on fashion and dress. I begin with Simmel (1971), who states that two social tendencies are necessary in order for fashion to exist. The first is union, the second isolation. Individuals must desire to be part of a larger whole (society), but they must also desire to be and to be considered as apart from that whole (Barnard 1996). Fashion is thus a unifying and differentiating force. For example, Beverley Skeggs (1997) clearly demonstrates how "respectable" working-class women differentiate themselves through "classy" clothes from working-class women who have "let themselves go," the unrespectable others against whom they come to identify themselves. On a more local level, Elizabeth Wilson states, "we want to look like our friends but not to be clones" (1992, 34, cited in Barnard 1996, 11). Thus, fashion affirms us as members of particular social groups, but the ideological maneuver (interpellation) of fashion forces us to misrecognize ourselves as individuals. Differentiation is thus important even within the group to which we are affiliated.

Academic writings on fashion have frequently emphasized the communicative meanings of the consumption and display of fashion and dress—too much, Colin Campbell (1996) argues. He is especially critical of certain postmodern writers (Baudrillard is implied) who attribute too much importance to the symbolic meaning of products and too little to the meaning of actions. He shows the ways in which postmodern writers who stress the playfulness of identity—the ways in which identities might be taken up and thrown off—implicitly align themselves with "economists and rational strategy theorists" (1996, 96), positioning consumption and display as a set of rational, unconstrained choices. Although there is some validity in this argument, he proceeds to adopt an opposite polemic, wherein *individuals* or *consumers* function almost unconsciously within a constrained set of choices. After so carefully differentiating between the symbolic meanings of goods and actions, he then tends to conflate them. For instance, he attributes the cleaning instructions on the labels of garments to actions, therefore divorcing ease of cleaning from the product's symbolic value. However, it is perhaps his homogenizing and feminizing assumptions about "individuals" involved in consuming fashion that are the most worrying: "a woman holds up a dress and says, 'this won't suit me, I am too small; it would look good on a taller woman,' or, another will say, 'round necklines don't suit me,' or 'I can't wear yellow, it doesn't suit my complexion' " (Campbell 1996, 102).

Using this framework effectively erases the social, rendering fashion a question of individual taste or "personal identity," and leaves little room for discussion of the visible manifestations of social identities. However, in my research it is clear that fashion's communicative role in the production of identities is an important one and must not be overlooked.

Having been invisible for so long in writing, the media, law, and culture more generally, as well as being literally invisible on the bodies of subjects (you can't tell by looking), queer identities have become visibilized through a number of mechanisms. The politics of visibility as well as the many everyday cues and codes of dress, gesture, or conduct are often used to communicate identity to others of the same or different groups. Butch and camp, to name but two, have become signs of sexuality (see Munt 1996; Nestle 1987) and are mapped onto the surface of bodies, not least through clothes. As Rosa Ainley comments, "Without visual identity there is no presence, and that means no social support networks, and no community" (1995, 122). Thus, Campbell's female consumer whose choice lies in whether it is the red or the blue frock that suits her most is irrelevant to strong social identities, if indeed she is relevant to anyone but Campbell's imaginary shoppers. Mort (1997) proposes a more sensible approach, suggesting that overgeneralizations are unhelpful in the field of consumption and that writers should focus on the specific. He also suggests, drawing on Giddens and Foucault, that consumption forms part of a project of the self, a significant part of social identity. This point is echoed in Elizabeth Wilson's work: "If . . . the self in all its aspects appears threatened in modern society, then fashion becomes an important—indeed vital—medium in the recreation of the lost self or 'decentred subject' . . . for the individual to lay claim to a particular style may be more than ever a lifeline, a proof that one does at least exist" (1985, 122).

Arguably, until the 1990s, fashion itself may have provided the most important signifier in the construction of queer identities. Gay men were marked simply by being fashionable against the backdrop of a masculinity (beyond temporary affiliation to specific youth subcultures) largely disinterested in a subject dismissed as the prevail of women. Lesbians, of course, visibly fought fashion as a constraining and feminizing force of capitalism and heteropatriarchy. However, the 1990s complicated matters. Androgeny, fashionable many times in history but most recently developed by lesbian and bisexual women, has slipped easily into the mainstream of youth culture more generally. Moreover, the media frenzy over "lesbian chic" (possibly fueled by panics over the erosion of visible differentiation between straight and queer women) has inspired some (middle-class) lesbians and bisexual women to reclaim fashion and to muscle in on some of the "boyz' fun" organized around the plethora of new clubs and bars, and facilitated by a newfound disposable income in the climate of greater opportunities for women. Furthermore, as Sean Nixon shows (1996), the recent growth of men's magazines such as *FHM* and *GQ* in the United Kingdom has reproduced fashion as an acceptable pastime for straight men. Thus, queer markers in the 1990s have become more subtle and sophisticated than the jeans and checked shirts advocated in the 1970s and have moved signification away from generic styles of dress onto the specifics of labels such as Levis, Adidas, Ted Baker, and Versace, to name a few. That is not to say, though, that these labels in themselves can be taken as reliable evidence of sexuality, only that in specific contexts they can hint in a particular direction—thus are the complexities of postmodern sexual (and other) identity performances.

Interpreting Identities

Social theorists often talk about the ontological and epistemological as if they are, in effect, separate categories—one is experience, the other academic theory (except, of course, for standpoint theorists, for whom being *is* knowing). However, as Beverley Skeggs points out, "Experiences are always in the process of interpretation (even if not in the form of critical reflexivity), as are the interpretative frameworks which are brought to bear upon them which enable classificatory frameworks to be built around them so that some experiences are classified as authentic and others as theoretical" (1997, 28). Thus, all experiences (and their interpretative frameworks) are mediated by discourses, by preexisting epistemologies. In this chapter, I focus on three epistemologies. I am aware that the term *epistemology* is usually used to refer simply to academic discourse, but I feel the term is helpful in referring also to other systems of knowledge, whether they be academic, political, or subcultural (i.e., popular wisdoms and knowledges).

By academic discourse, I am referring to queer theory, something that needs no definition here. This discourse is distinct from what I refer to as political epistemology. Although such political discourses do tend to borrow from academic positions (inevitably because identity politics has traditionally forefronted the concerns of white, middle-class academics), the political level is inadequate because it tends to focus instead on the creation of specious binaries that are inevitably undermined. I return to this point later, but the binaries of sex and gender, being and acting, "in" and "out" (of the closet) are specific examples on which I focus. On a most basic level, for example, coming out and being out is not a simple, once-and-for-all position; it is context specific and processual (Seidman 1998; Valentine 1993b). Finally, then, the subcultural epistemology is an interpretative framework based around everyday popular knowledges circulating within queer subcultures. In particular, this subcultural epistemology tends to be characterized by essentialist notions of identity.

To illustrate the disjuncture between these epistemologies, Lisa Duggan (1995b) tells an anecdote about Eve Sedgwick and a "fact checker" from *Rolling Stone* who must make extraordinary conversational contortions in order to try and ascertain Sedgwick's sexuality (without particular success). Duggan uses the anecdote to illustrate "the gap between the predominantly contructivist language of queer studies and the essentialist presumptions of public discourse" (1995a, 183). To add a bit of weight to this argument, one has only to witness the appeal of Simon Le Vay's "gay brain" work (see Hegarty 1997) or of "immutability" arguments (Currah 1995) and attempts to see gays as a "quasi-ethnic group." Increasingly, such arguments are playing a role in U.S. and U.K. liberal political discourse.

Perhaps these different ways of speaking (in and out of the academy) can never truly resonate with each other, and queer theory can be taken up only partially in the realm of politics. Witness Judith Butler's displeasure in *Bodies That Matter* (1993) at the way in which *Gender Trouble* (1990) was misread and transformed into the political slogan "All Gender Is Drag!" Crucially, we need to assess the extent to which these discourses do or don't map onto one another. These matters are important if theorists continue to be concerned with the ways in which their particular messages are read for political and identity purposes. I argue, ultimately, that although poststructuralist academic discourse is rarely taken up in any meaningful way at either the level of the political or of the subcultural, it remains the most convincing way of conceptualizing the processes involved in the formation of identity.

Before I move on to the main body of the chapter, I would briefly like to illustrate the three levels of interpretation through an extract from one of my respondents, when she talked about an issue that was currently important to her as an executive member of a women's center. All members of the center were discussing the issue of transgender women and their access to the center, which would then be put to a vote. Reading this issue from a poststructuralist angle, we might conclude that because there is no "women's experience" and that in any case because gender is performative and the sexed body simply a product of gender discourse, there is no logical reason to exclude transgender women. Second-wave feminist theory, however, was quick to condemn transgender women's involvement in "women's space" and feminist politics (see, for example, Stone 1991). "We had this discussion and loads of the women there we going 'No, no, we can't have them in. It's got to be women born women. They're men, they're brought up men, and they don't share women's experience of oppression. It's got to be a safe space for women. There's the whole issue of men's violence!' And I think, 'What are we afraid of? A load of bloody men in frocks! Most of us there are twice the size of them.' " In this case, the outcome was that transgender women were voted in to the women's center, thus aligning subcultural discourses and queer theory if not exactly in rhetoric, then at least in political aim and outcome.

Uniform Identities

It is with these conflicts between everyday and theoretical explanations in mind that I began the study of video diaries. Perhaps the most interesting issue to emerge from this process—after I read accounts of the decentered, reflexive, performative self in the theoretical literature—was exactly the *lack* of reflexivity that many participants displayed in examining their self-presentations. This lack was slightly uneven depending on the context, as one might expect. For example, participants were very sensitive to the demands placed on them by uniforms and dress codes at work, but far less self-conscious when it came to their "leisure wear." Here, too, though, was a clear difference between "going out" clothes and "slobbing around" clothes worn only in the home.

"Dressing" is intricately linked to queer employment patterns throughout contemporary history. There are many recent rediscoveries of women who cross-dressed or lived as men in the nineteenth century in order to pursue male careers that were not open to them as women. Some were not discovered to be women until their postmortem examinations (sometimes prompting difficult explanations from their wives). During the first half of the twentieth century, especially at the time of the two world wars, the armed forces created opportunities and possibilities for queer men and women to earn money and leave home, to inhabit single-sex spaces, and to engage in non-sex-specific occupations.

Uniforms can also alleviate some of the problems of dressing. For example, one respondent in Rosa Ainley's study explains:

> I didn't realize at the time, when I went into nursing, how much I would hide behind the uniform and how comfortable I felt in a traditional female role, where I could be totally hidden. Never mind that I used to walk with a bit of a sway or anything like that, I was in a dress with a little cap perched on my head. It wasn't really until I left the health service for another job that I realized I did not know how to dress, I did not know how I wanted to look. Or I did know how I wanted to look, but might well be accused of being lesbian and that bothered me. (1995, 137)

Uniforms can thus be a mask (experienced either positively or negatively) or a marker of sexual identity. Even now, uniforms (those for sailors and police officers, for example) have a certain affectionate place in lesbian, gay, and bisexual cultures, and lesbians continue to be attracted by careers in the army, police force, and prison service, for example (Ainley 1995). However, outside of these occupations, dress codes can cause problems, and there is much evidence to suggest that such problems may be one reason why lesbians, gay men, and bisexuals gravitate toward occupations or institutions where nonhegemonic sexualities are more accepted or where equal opportunities policies are firmly in place. Although this preference has, of course, much to do with other kinds of restrictions or discriminations, the freedom to "express" one's sexuality or to "be oneself" at work is frequently cited as a motivation in choosing particular forms of employment, especially in the "pink economy," for example.

Diarists in this study recognize work clothes as restraining or empowering in different ways. Seb is a bisexual psychiatric nurse in his early thirties. He lives with his partner Gill (also in nursing) in a large communal house shared with six others in a city in the English Midlands. Both he and his partner are nonmonogamous and have relationships with other men and women. Jo is a lesbian and a hospital technician who lives with her partner Sue (a trainee teacher) in a former council house in a small southern Midlands town. Neither Seb nor Jo are "out" at work.

Both are obliged to wear uniforms at work, but actually subvert these uniforms to a greater or lesser degree. In both cases, they are required not to wear jeans, which they both *do* wear (although they wear only black and not blue ones). Jo is also required to wear a white tunic top, which she does but always covers over with a jumper or sweatshirt. Seb is not required to wear a tie but has to wear "a shirt which would facilitate the wearing of a tie." To this requirement he responds by wearing a collarless shirt. He is not required to wear sedate colors, but all his workmates do so. He prefers to wear bright colors: green, red, or orange shirts and brightly colored trousers.[2]

Steve is gay and the part-time manager of a clothing shop. He is in his early twenties and also studies law at a local university. He lives at home with his parents but has a partner, Patrick, at whose house he spends much of his time. At work, Steve is obliged to wear suits from the store's range. He thus has separate wardrobes for work and for leisure, one comprising dark suits and the other brighter and much more varied attire. He explains:

> People who join the job don't necessarily know I'm gay. It is never necessarily spoken about. Everyone knows. Me and my close friends there go

2. Many bisexual men seem to prefer brightly colored clothes, tie-dye especially, which is interesting because this preference can be read as a critique of heteromasculine dress codes, perhaps a more critical position than that of gay men. I would suggest that this critique is owing to bisexual men's political connections with feminism (through their closer contact with often politicized women) and with the men's movement.

to clubs together, and they all know Patrick; he comes in every week; it
isn't a problem. But it does make you far more firm. The job itself requires
that, but in terms of sexual identity, people don't necessarily associate
that firmness with a gay man. . . . I think you should dress appropriately
for what the occasion is, but hopefully the person has the good sense to
apply their individualism to what they're wearing. . . . [I]t's part of the
job, and you have to accept it. . . . I quite enjoy the whole feeling it gives to
you of authority and control and feeling that you were dressed properly
for the job.

He feels that it is appropriate to his position to wear the suits and enjoys
the aura of power and respectability they give him. He explains at another
point (which his sister corroborates in the diary) that he is much sterner at
work and that the formal clothes help him assert his authority in his
workplace.

Steve is less critical of his "uniform" than Jo and Seb because it gives
back the authority he lacks in the potentiality of having his sexuality
equated with a weaker management style. Further, the suits are not a uniform per se and can be selected from a range, which allows an element of
"individual expression" through choice, disguising to a certain extent the
nature of his organization's control of his body. For Jo, Seb, and Steve, then,
the "tampering" they do with their uniforms is seen as a battle for "individuality" within a homogenized workplace. For example, Seb says, "Although I don't think that the clothes I wear are an expression of my
sexuality, as my confidence with my sexuality has increased, my clothes
have become brighter. I don't think my clothes say that I'm bisexual, but
they do reflect my confidence in my identity." This statement is interesting
because, of course, it is not just sexuality that creates "individuals" in the
workplace. One has to look no further than the university to find examples
of eccentric professors who create a certain individual style (which tends to
conform to the romantic rather than derogatory sense of *eccentric*). However, in Seb's case, his "individuality" is clearly tied to his sexual identity;
thus, although he has not expressed it categorically, he feels individual to
the (presumed) monolithic heterosexuality of his workplace. That this "individuality" is expressed through the wearing of colors is thus unsurprising given that heteromasculinity's uniform is grey, navy, or black. As Linda
McDowell (1997) shows, there is extreme pressure on both male and female workers in financial institutions to conform to specific color codes.

Women who wear bright colors are mistaken for secretaries, and thus conformity to preexisting (masculine) color codes for stockmarket traders is imperative to maintain their status within the workplace. For men (and women in male domains), strict regimes of bodily regulation (including the disguising of any involuntary weight loss or gain) are a prerequisite in the display of self-control and self-discipline that mark out potential "high flyers."

Furthermore, Jo suggests that dress codes would certainly have an impact on what kind of job she might apply for: "I could never get a job where I would have to deal with the public. That would mean skirts and frocks and high-heeled shoes and I'm not the kind of person that spends hours in front of the mirror in the morning." Thus, her nonidentification with the conventional patterns of femininity, combined with her recognition of the way in which these patterns are exploited in the interactive service encounter, might prevent her from making certain career choices. This point is important because her comment is not about a definite choice, from the position of sexual identification, to work in the pink economy, but rather a (somewhat essentialistic) notion of the incompatibility between subcultural dress codes and certain kinds of feminine employment practice. More positively, we might attribute this choice to the lesbian-feminist discourses around the construction of heterosexual femininity and to the adoption of a political position that rejects this performance.

Carl, a gay male nurse working in HIV and AIDS information and care says:

> I get up at seven most days to get ready for work. This is what I wear, just the usual shirt-and-tie jobby [sic]; I prefer white shirts as they look smarter. I'd prefer to be wearing a suit, but I don't actually have the money to buy a decent suit, so I just wear a shirt and tie. I wear this because it's smarter. A lot of gay men doing my sort of work in the community—for example, a friend of mine tends to wear Adidas T-shirts and a pair of jeans, and that's what he feels comfortable in, but I don't, I don't feel comfortable in that sort of stuff . . . except on a Friday, when I tend to dress down a little bit as it's the start of the weekend.

Not everyone is able to "power dress" in the way that Steve describes, even if it is what they desire. For Carl, wearing good suits to work is simply not an option given his access to economic capital. Thus, we must not forget that the performance of identity is frequently far from the ideal one we might like to portray and is often constrained by limited access to disposable income.

Identification with the attire of the workplace, then, is largely expressed negatively in the examples I have used to represent the broader theme. But clothing used to express identity in leisure time is viewed much more favorably and much less reflexively. Several of the respondents, when dressing in their "going out" or "staying in" clothes, express the ideal of "comfort" as the primary motivation in their choice of these clothes—that they chose the clothes that they were wearing because these clothes are the most comfortable. In some cases, participants are completely unable to add anything to this description and motive for buying and wearing these clothes, and here lies the key to the (limited) possibilities of identity performances I hope to explore. Also, the participants make some attempt to pass over the question of "labels" of clothing that clearly had social meanings in specific contexts at the time of writing. The clearest example is when Jo explains the purchase of an "original" Adidas tracksuit top. She expresses the motive for this purchase as being comfort and liking the look of the white stripes down the sleeves. At this point in the diary, her partner is moved to contribute to the question by explaining that in fact Jo had seen a "gorgeous babe" in a trendy gay bar wearing an identical top. After this encounter, it had taken an extended tour of a rag market twenty miles away to find a similar top (importantly a secondhand one from the first time that such tops had been fashionable). Thus, what Jo describes as an acquisition for comfort, her partner now assures us was a highly inconvenient purchase precipitated by a fleeting flirtation in a highly specific location. Jo later confirms this explanation: "I think I look at other clothes that other people wear, and if they look nice and comfortable, then I choose to wear them. I mean I saw a woman in [a gay bar] that had an Adidas top on, and it really suited her, it looked really nice . . . so that's probably why I choose to wear Adidas tops. . . . Plus she was damn sexy [laughs]." The *social* meaning of this purchase is perhaps reinforced through a quote from Carl. He is about the same age as Jo and also frequents "trendy" gay bars: "I wear trainers now, rather than boots. Adidas trainers, very important, because they're quite fashionable at the moment, and if you're going to be accepted on the scene, you've got to dress right."

The Politics of Comfort

The discourse on comfort therefore has both political and subcultural connotations rather than a simple appeal to some essentialistic or "natural" notion. In a sense, it is this element that signifies above all others for my diarists the complexity of the formation of identities. If, rather than dismissing diarists' explanations around comfort, we deconstruct them, using clues from elsewhere in the video diaries, an interesting picture of the differences between academic and popular discourses emerges, and this picture can be conceptualized most effectively within an ontological/epistemological framework. Of course, on one level, these statements represent a recourse to physical comfort—but is this phenomenon neutral? What is it that the discourse of comfort conveys?

Comfort as Nature

First, comfort embodies *resistance* to the hegemonic discourses of "proper" feminine behavior and attire. Lesbian and bisexual feminism has, as Judith Butler (1990) describes, been quick to point out that it is *culture* that demands femininity. If femininity is imposed by patriarchal culture and is socially constructed, then it can be changed. Thus, first—and second-wave feminisms retain a binary system of gender and sex, where gender is implicitly assumed to follow sex. Feminism's rejection of patriarchal claims has been the rejection of traditional femininity, but also a replacement of it with notions of women's *nature*—for example, cooperative and nonhierarchical relationships with other women, women's connectedness to the earth and to "Mother Nature," and so on.[3] This discourse has reproduced itself on the surface of the body as a return to the natural body—the giving up of the shaving of legs and armpits, the wearing of makeup, the adopting of fashion. In this project, then, appeals to comfort become appeals to the "nature" of feminism—that is, the rejection of *(unnatural)* femininity.

Butler undoes this particular version of feminism by referring back to

3. Of course, this view is a very white, Western notion of woman, which in its romanticism of nature excludes women who might envisage their emancipation in escape from such a connection.

de Beauvoir, who famously asserted "one is not born a woman, but rather one becomes one." To take this statement to its logical conclusion, there is no guarantee that all those born female will become women or that those born male won't. In short, there is no reason to believe that gender will follow sex or that the binaries of sex and gender will remain as binaries. Thus, in its appeal to nature and comfort, second-wave feminism actually closes down the possibilities of gendered (subject) and sexual (object choice) identities. Appeals to comfort are complicit in this restriction of possible identities through their implicit fixing of "true" gender to the "natural" body: what is comfortable for the lesbian could not be comfortable for the "false" (feminine or transgendered) subject and vice versa. This restriction, filtering into lesbian and bisexual subjectivity, stems from an originally emancipatory feminist political project—perhaps as its unintended consequences.

For men, however, the rejection of accepted patterns of masculinity may mean subjecting themselves to exactly the technologies of the body from which feminists have struggled to emancipate women:

> I'm shaving my legs [on camera]. Because I get quite long hair on my legs, and gay men don't like that. At least I don't anyway. And I don't feel comfortable with it. . . . This is an important part, I s'pose, of me and my identity. In that, I don't feel comfortable being me if I've got quite long hair, because I do get quite long hair, all over really, on my arms and legs and chest. I don't know if you can see [pulls up arm hairs to demonstrate]. And the image at the moment is quite young and fit and smooth. So you feel quite out of it if you're not young and fit and smooth. And as I'm not young and fit, the closest I'm going to get is smooth. I cut my hair really, not shave it; if I ever get a body, as in muscles and stuff, I might get my chest waxed. But at the moment I can't see the point in spending all that money, because I don't show my body, and I'm not going to show my body until I feel comfortable with it. That's one of the problems of being gay I suppose. (Carl)

In this quote, the dynamic of comfort is quite clearly contradictory; although Carl does not feel "comfortable" going out on the scene unless he attends to his body, he is quite clearly uncomfortable about having to do so.

Comfort Inside and Out

Comfort also signifies the comfort one might feel from the degree of fit between outside of one's body and its inside, the way in which identity is mapped onto the body. Comfort means in this case that one expresses externally that which one feels inside. As Carol-Anne Tyler writes,

> As signifiers of our selves with which we are deeply identified, we wish our name and our image to transparently reflect our being, like an iconic sign, and to be existentially or naturally bound to it, like an index. Such signs are supposed to be "motivated" rather than "arbitrary" or conventional and artificial, and therefore less susceptible to the disarticulations of signifier and signified, sign and referent, which make communication confusing. (1994, quoted in Fraser 1997, 43)

In other words, there is a wish to close the gap between performance (acting) and ontology (being), a desire to be self-present to both oneself and others. Comfort in this case derives from being "recognizably" queer to both oneself and others. In part, this notion is informed by the politics of visibility. As a discursive absence, lesbians and bisexual women must enforce their presence through the communication of signs, which cannot be left to the chance conversation or discovery but must rather be signified (through butch, for instance), where signifiers are fixed to an ontological truth of being.

Here again, first- and second-wave feminist and lesbian politics assert a binary: the binary of being and acting—the self and its performance. For example, Marilyn Frye writes: "being lesbian [and] being heterosexual are not simply matters of sexual preference or bodily behaviours. They are complex matters of attachment, orientation in the world, vision, habits, or communication and community. . . . In my own case, being lesbian is an attitude evolved over perhaps fifteen years . . . It would have been 'inauthentic' to act the lesbian in certain ways too early in that process. It now would be inauthentic not to, in certain ways and certain situations" (1985, quoted in Fraser 1997, 43). Thus, although feminists set up the binary of acting and being, there is still an implication that acting *follows* being and is thus part of it. Mariam Fraser shows how the bisexual woman disrupts this logic in that she is considered inauthentic: she acts like a lesbian but is not one. As with sex and gender, then, feminism sets up a binary, which is only to be fixed as signifier and signified. The binary is really two sides of the same coin where the cultural mirrors the biological. Feminist political logic once again reinstates the essentialism of the recourse, in this case not to the body but to the self, so it is unsurprising that the comfort expressed by our diarists locates the comfort of identity in the individual body, reinstating the notion of the expressive individual. The essentializing of comfort through the homology of acting and being once again prescribes exclusive sexuality. If acting following being represents the authentic, then acts that are not located in the body or identity are clearly inauthentic. Thus, with lesbian feminism, the bisexual and transgendered (among others) are inauthentic copies of the authentic lesbian self.

In appealing to the comfort one feels about this homology, therefore, what is being masked in popular discourse is the very *performativity* of that identity—its creation through a discourse of power. The choice of comfortable clothes proposes identity as a "natural phenomenon," giving identity an essentialism that therefore assists heterosexuality in retaining a false binary. It covers up the "construction" of identity and therefore masks its historical roots as a discourse, closing down other potential positions or movements within that discourse. Foucault and Butler are both quick to point out that all discourses, not just hegemonic ones, are located in power. All definitions (identities and representations) are exclusive. As Butler says, "identity categories tend to be instruments of regulatory regimes, whether as the normalizing categories of oppressive structures or as the rallying points for a liberatory contestation of that very oppression. . . . To propose that the invocation of identity is always a risk [of being recolonized under the sign of lesbian] does not imply that resistance to it is always or only symptomatic of a self-inflicted homophobia" (1990, 13–14).

Under heterosexuality, then, the constitution of desire requires the production and institution of oppositions between femininity and masculinity, where they are expressions of female and male, which means that certain identities cannot exist—where gender does not follow from sex and where practices of desire do not follow from either sex or gender. Thus, compulsory heterosexuality is maintained. The causal relationship between sex, gender, and desire is formed with desire expressing gender and gender expressing desire. The *effect* of heterosexuality becomes a *cause* of sex and gender. The persistence of "abnormal" categories exposes the regulatory frameworks of the discourse of heterosexuality. But the criticism of heterosexual desire in rendering itself exclusive in relation to sex and gender must therefore also be a criticism of homosexual desire and therefore of identity because sexual identity is characterized as desire. Even bisexuality assumes the binary of sex—having sex with *both* sexes, which is why many more radical bisexual political groups are reorganizing around the term *polysexual* (or around the slide into "I'm not bisexual, just sexual").

Crafting a sexual position, Butler says, is therefore about exclusion (of what one is not) and thus involves becoming haunted by precisely that which is excluded. The more rigid the position, the greater the ghost (homosexuality for heterosexuality, bisexuality for homosexuality). Homosexuality is dismissed as a copy of heterosexuality (butch and femme stereotypes, and "pretended families," for example), but because heterosexuality defines itself precisely in opposition to homosexuality, then heterosexuality renders itself a copy of a copy: "Heterosexuality can only be understood as a compulsive and compulsory repetition that can only produce the *effect* of its own originality" (Butler 1991, 21, emphasis in original). This constant and repetitive performance—a series of acts, gestures, and enactments mapped onto the surface of the body—produces but never reveals identity. There is no inner truth of identity, just a fantasy inscribed on the surface of the body. Again, however, it is not just heterosexual identity that is performative.

Once identity is understood only as performativity divorced from any notion of an essential self or of individual truth, multiple identity positions or identity fictions become possible, or at least plausible. Thus, the fixing of comfort to the expressive individual self denies the performativity of identity and thus the transgressive possibilities of the disruption of that performance. Though Butler is quick to point out that performativity is not voluntary or arbitrary, the recognition of identity as performative does offer possibilities for its subversion.

Performing Bodies

In the video diaries, a number of respondents talked about a certain "discomfort" when going out "on the scene." This discomfort tended to be expressed as a feeling of being watched or stared at—not being "cruised" but being in some sense "evaluated." In fact, Jo says that she sometimes feels more comfortable in "straight" spaces than in queer ones, and Carl talks at length about wanting to wear clothes that he feels unable to wear on the scene because he does not have the necessary muscular body on which to wear "skimpy" items of clothing:

> This is what I plan to wear. It's all black, which makes me feel comfortable because it slims me down. I feel a bit chubby. Although I quite fancy the blue, which is very clingy and tends to show any lumps, and as I've got them, I don't think I'll wear that. This is what I want to wear one day. It's my favorite top ever. I've never worn this out yet. It's wonderful. I bought it in the gay part of New York—Greenwich Village. I think that it's really nice, I love this, but I don't actually wear it so far, basically because I don't think I've really got the body for it, so until I feel comfortable wearing that, it'll be going back to the wardrobe. But hopefully by the end of this month I'll be able to wear it.

This gaze is not one of desire, then, but rather a disciplinary gaze, a policing of body shapes and styles of dress, which leaves several of the respondents feeling some kind of inadequacy in what they consider to be "their own" spaces. As Lurie explains, "the concept of 'proper dress' is totally dependent on situation. To wear the costume considered 'proper' for a situation acts as a sign of involvement in it, and the person whose clothes do not conform to these standards is likely to be more or less subtly excluded from participation" (1981, 13).

The diarists' accounts make clear the power at work within the so-called emancipatory discourses of queer, which does not imply that the discourses of lesbian and gay culture are as destructive as homophobic ones (it is unlikely that one would get beaten up for poor fashion sense), but they are powerful and do exert disciplinary technologies on the bodies of their subjects. These technologies in turn produce perfomativities of lesbian and gay identities that locate their performance exactly in the idea of the biological or psychological self. As Lauren Berlant puts it, poststructuralist theorists "have shown how sexuality is the modern form of self-intelligibility: I am my identity; my identity is fundamentally sexual; and my practices reflect that (and if they don't, they require submission to sexual science, self-help, or other kinds of laws)" (1997, 17). She also says, though, that bisexuality has not made it fully into "the sexual star system" because it is difficult to *express* bisexuality. Similarly, Fraser argues that because bisexuality has been largely absent from queer discourse, then bisexuals may not be subject to the same disciplinary technologies of the self as lesbians and gays. However, as one bisexual diarist who was becoming disillusioned with the "bisexual scene" says, "If I meet one more man with a beard, dressed in tie dye, who wants to hug me, I shall be sick." Clearly, then, regulatory frameworks of dress, gesture, and even facial hair do exist in bisexual networks, implying that there may be much the same disciplinary technologies exerted on the body within bisexuality as elsewhere.

Yet again, the political, in setting up a binary of oppressive (bad) heterosexuality and liberatory (good) homosexuality, reifies the signifier of the emancipatory lesbian and gay (and to some extent bisexual) culture. What this reification effectively creates is a situation in which participants in queer culture have no language or concepts with which to express their discomfort at certain times. Instead of affording a recognition of the hierarchical power relations that exist within the culture, and thus a way to verbalize and transgress some of its more regulatory aspects or perhaps even to lobby for change, people often resort to dismissing, for example, the "bitchiness of the scene" or to setting up alternative gay groups such as gay conservatives and nonscene or antiscene groups. Such maneuvers once again individualize sexual subjects as both the individual self made uncomfortable by queer culture and the individuals who make one feel uncomfortable. They in effect may prevent exactly what lesbian, gay, and bisexual politics hopes to achieve—the collective emancipation of its members—through the fracturing and splintering of the queer political community (one only has to look at the disintegration and fracturing of queer politics in the late 1980s to see what this means in practice).

Social Identities, Individual Selves?

This brings me to another point about the empirical material presented in this chapter—that the link between the comfort of the outside of the body with the "naturalness" of the inside prioritizes the individual over the social. Individuality is stressed in opposition to the uniform of work, but also in relation to the "uniform of queer." The misrecognition of oneself as an individual in opposition to uniform, fashion, and subculture denies the place of the social in the construction of identity positions. In Jo's case, for example, her choice of tracksuit top is clearly one of *social* meaning. The desire to purchase and wear this top was the result of a social interaction in a queer location. Her inspiration in her choice of dress, far from deriving from within herself (as she suggests), comes from a kind of queer aesthetic with which she identifies. This queer aesthetic is always social; outside of the social, it has no meaning. Within the social, it signifies her comfort, physical but also aesthetic—comfort in reflecting her identity, but also in being able to express it.

Thus, although the popular discourse of lesbigay culture locates sexuality in the individual, the social is always important in its development. The scene may be "uncomfortable" for certain people at certain times, but it is not only here that the social operates. For many people, most discussion about their sexuality takes place in the "comfort" of the home, rather than in the frenetic atmosphere of "the scene." This apparently "private" space is thus key in the *social* construction of sexual identities. At rest, as opposed to at play, performative strategies may be less intense—or at least deflected from the body onto the home itself. All of the lesbians, bisexuals, and gay men in the diaries use signifiers of identity in their interior decor; for example, Jo uses posters of lesbian icons such as kd lang and Jodie Foster, a poster of a naked woman with a large whip, as well as lesbian safer sex posters produced by the Terrance Higgins Trust. Carl says that his Patsy Cline, Bananarama, Madonna, Janet Jackson, and Eurovision CDs are indicative of his sexuality. Seb's house includes a cross-dressed mannequin as a central feature of his decor. Even Steve, who lives with his parents, has a tacit understanding with them that his bedroom is a private space that his father should not enter. His walls are adorned with posters of River Phoenix, Madonna, and other gay icons, along with photographs of his boyfriend.

This is not to say that in the home one returns to a private backstage self, but rather that social interaction may be less instrumental in terms of projecting one's sex appeal or fun-loving nature, which may be required on "the scene." I would also refrain from making blanket statements about the privacy and security of the home, however. This issue is much more complicated than popular discourses suggest. Carl, for instance, found it necessary to turn up his music while talking about nonmonogamy on the video diary. He apologizes for the sound quality but explains that because his flatmates know his boyfriend Kieran, and because Kieran does not approve of nonmonogamy, if they were to overhear Carl's more positive views, they might pass on the information. Furthermore, Carl had in the past had a relationship with the man he now lives with, who is now married and living with his wife in the same shared house. Neither his former boyfriend's wife nor Carl's current boyfriend know about this relationship, which he suggests does at times cause some discomfort. For many people, then, the home may not be a "safe" place of refuge; as Johnston and Valentine (1995) show, lesbians living in the family home may be at best encouraged to perform heterosexuality, at worst physically harmed by family members for failing to do so. Furthermore, the lesbian home may come under the pressure of surveillance by neighbors (who may overhear through badly soundproofed walls or overlook from the garden fence or window) and by visiting family members, for which "de-dyking" strategies may be required—removing signifiers (and signifieds) from the home in preparation for such visits. The overprotected home risks the insularization of the lesbian relationship, creating additional pressures and feelings of confinement and social exclusion, and possibly domestic violence. Turning the home into a largely social space where visitors are frequent can also have its disadvantages, reinstating the pressures of lesbian performance through surveillance from other lesbians. As Johnston and Valentine state, " 'Political correctness,' which has come to haunt the lesbian feminist landscape, or other 'othodoxies,' can be invoked by some women to regulate the performative aspects of others' lesbian identities within the domestic environment" (1995, 109).

However, in most cases, for the diarists, home was the place that they *experienced* as most comfortable, where they could "slob out," wear comfortable clothes (not neutral clothes in terms of their identities, but perhaps less-communicative ones). In one's home, one most often has at least some control over who enters, with whom one spends time, and how one's habitus is organized. Also, issues of sexual identity might be deflected by the day-to-day things with which all householders must deal—paying bills, cooking and eating, and in some cases taking care of children. The diarists also highlight these aspects of their lives. That is not to say, though, that at home one becomes an individualized self. In fact, even in the choice of home, some aspect of identity is called into play, not only in the type of home, but also importantly its location. Especially for middle-class respondents, there was some effort to find homes close to other lesbian, bisexual, or gay households. In one case, some friends—a lesbian couple and a gay man—had moved in next door to one another. Also, for a lesbian respondent with children, living in a catchment area for a school that employed equal opportunity policies for the children of lesbian parents was an important factor in the choice of the location of her home. The choice of house, its interior decor, the way in which queer identities are expressed within the home, then, are not *individualized*, private decisions but rather highly *social* ones.

Thus, although the diarists inevitably draw on essentialist logics to locate their sexuality, at least one lesbian diarist resists some of the more rigid aspects of lesbian political discourse. Her answerphone message announces, "Hi, we're out having liposuction at the moment. Only glamorous people can leave a message after the tone!" with riotous background laughter. This resistence does not preclude a rejection of femininity in styles of dress or gesture; instead it indicates the multiple discourses with respect to which subjects negotiate their identities, borrowing from hegemonic, feminist, and lesbian political discourses as well as from those of gay culture. One could read this answerphone message as an example of lesbian camp (see Graham 1995). It is in the interplay of different discourses and social spaces, including the home, that people come to negotiate and formulate "comfortable" identities.

These "comfortable identities" might be equated with Foucault's ideas on the care of the self. *The Care of the Self* provides an ethics that guides the subject in different spatial spheres or contexts. This work is done in the interplay of the "soul" (the part of the self that lies beyond discourse) that one might access through private contemplation, the social, and the political. For Elspeth Probyn (1995b), it is the interplay of the ontological and epistemological. The ontological may provide the ground from which to reject the political, like Johnson and Valentine's respondents. But so might the political (epistemological) provide the vantage point from which to recognize one's ontological conditions as part of a system of domination. Probyn gives the example of the "sudden shock of recognition" of one's condition, seeing through the ideological discourses that otherwise mask and prevent this recognition. It is perhaps this process that occurs in Seb's earlier statement that wearing bright colors as he becomes more confident with his sexuality marks his "individuality" in his workplace. Through political discourses on sexuality, Seb recognizes himself as an "individual" in a workplace that is hegemonically heterosexual, which in turn produces an ethics of the self that generates a bodily critique of the hegemonic norm. Bright clothes, as one aspect of his performative identity, help display his sexuality to those in the know, but are also a political statement and critique of the rigid dress codes enforced by heteronormativity. The body is politicized in line with the social and political soul. Thus, though Seb clearly has the possibility of acknowledging his sexuality, while simultaneously conforming to conventional dress codes at work or alternatively coming out and sporting a T-shirt, he negotiates these oppositional discourses and creates an ethics of the self that aligns his body with his soul, ensuring that, rather than the performance of separate identities in different spaces, there is in fact a high degree of continuity of identity in moving between them. Similarly, Jo clearly believes that she performs her lesbian identity at work without having to "come out" in the political sense. Both Jo and Seb stress that they do nothing to hide their sexualities at work. For example, in Jo's video diary, the camera pans around her workspace, focusing on two photographs of partially clad or naked 1920s-style women pinned up on the wall next to her desk. She explains:

> Even with pictures like that on the wall, people still have no idea. You can be almost blatant, and people still don't know. I never talk about men. I never talk about boyfriends. Whatever I do, that seems to be OK. Although I haven't told anybody here, there seems to be almost an understanding that I am [a lesbian]. I think they know, but nothing is ever said. But then again, sometimes they say some really homophobic things, and I think they couldn't possibly know. But sometimes I say things to people here, and I think I'm really surprised I get away with it. Sometimes it's really filthy, and I keep doing it. And I think sometime or other they're bound to get an idea, but they just don't.

In this way, responsibility for being "out" is shifted from herself (the author of her bodily text) to her colleagues (her readers). If they cannot recognize the signs of her identity, then her failure to be out is in effect their fault, a product of their stupidity rather than of her own lack of courage (as some more rigid political discourses might suggest). Again we can see a close alignment between postmodern theories of identity and everyday lived experiences and expectations.

The Body as Text

Thus, identity is spread over the surface of the body, the outward text of the inner ethics of the self. As Elizabeth Grosz explains, drawing on Derrida's discussion of the signature, "the paradoxical and divided position of the subject in and beyond the text, involves the necessary and irreducible trace of the one within the other, the implication of the text's outside with its inside, and of its inside with establishing its borders and thus the outside, in short, its fundamentally folded, 'invaginated' character" (1995, 20). The text is thus not irreducibly specific—the product of a unique individuality—but rather is always capable of "being reduced from a proper name to a common noun, becoming the content of an utterance. . . . The trace of the signature, then, cannot simply be identified with the proprietary mark of the author; instead it is an effect of the text's mode of materiality, the fact that as a product the text is an effect of a *labor*, a work on and with signs, a collaborative (even if hostile) labor of writing and reading" (Grosz 1995, 20).

Thus, the inscription on the body of the text of a subject's identity is an individual inscription (authorial propriety) that also at once signs the subject as a product of other (external social identity) texts. This is Derrida's notion of the signature, a binding together of the author as both creator of a text but also product of text. In the sense in which the body is a text, identity is always inscribed socially, although this inscription will have differing manifestations as the body's author attempts to inscribe proprietorial meaning. According to this sense, then, the queer body is the signature of queer textuality. It is not static or constant, but is shifting, like the signature, never manifesting itself twice in identical ways, yet at the same time carrying the mark of both its author and the texts that produce it. Card's outline of Aristotle's notion of "family resemblance" is useful here (1985, quoted in Fraser 1997, 51). The term *resemblance* can be applied to anything that is called by the same name but does not possess any one characteristic in common. Although Card uses this term in a rather different way (in proving bisexuality's inauthenticity), I think the term is useful to look at the relationship between authors, signatures, and texts in relation to the body.

Elspeth Probyn sees this thing that I have called "family resemblance" as an ensemble of images written on the body through the Deleuzean notion of productive desire: "The similarity of bodies, is a matter not of similar origins but rather is compelled by a similarity of desire to arrange one's body, to queer oneself through movement. As I see the configuration of my body as image on her body, I also can feel the configuration of hers on mine. However, this is not a constant or immediate fact; it has to be made, to be configured through the desire to conjoin images" (1995, 15). This configuration is not total, however. Not all lesbians desire all lesbians (or look like all lesbians); rather it is the social configuration in conjunction with the individual signature mapped onto the body, or onto parts of the body, that marks out individual desires—something in the interplay, as Probyn puts it, between bodies and representations. Thus, queer identities are constructed family resemblances not mapped onto the body in identical ways; they might be more or less subtle; they are mediated by the physicality of bodies, by the interplay of other identities and by the appropriateness of dress codes for particular spaces. This is the strength of the family resemblance—its versatility; it is not a uniform through which all its members are unequivocally marked for all audiences.

But still, this is only half (or less) of the story—a story is created not only by writers, but by readers. Any bodily text can covey its intended meaning only if its readers read it in the way the author requires. Family resemblances can be spotted only by those who "know" the "family." Meaning is constructed by readers of texts, not by writers of them, and therefore there are infinite possibilities for the queer body to be misread. A short anecdote from one diarist illustrates this point exactly. He was at college, arriving late to class one day:

> I walked in, and this bunch of girls were going "Martin's gay, Martin's gay"—Martin is this straight guy in our class. And Martin says, "Yes, and for all you know Steve [the respondent] could be my lover." And the girls said, "Oh, don't be stupid, we *know* Steve isn't gay; you're the one who's gay because you're obsessed with your appearance, always looking in the mirror." So I said, *"Au contraire!"* and gave them my big "I am gay" speech because I've worked hard for this reputation, and I'm not about to lose it. And they said, "Oh Steve, you're so funny, you're such a wit and a wag; I've told my parents all about you!" . . . They wouldn't believe me!

Steve says this last sentence with absolute incredulity. For him, and for many others, his gay identity is clearly coded and marked on his body, yet for his fellow students, who lacked the subcultural capital to decode his performative identity, his body was read "against the text." This misreading causes Steve amusement, but also dismay. There is an extreme discomfort in being read against one's signature (his reputation, which he has worked hard for). His straight audience's misreading of cultural codes invoked a reaction in which Steve attempted to refix the meaning of his bodily text, supplementing it with the intertextuality of gay political and ontological discourses. When this attempt too was misread, the discomfort of the lack of homology between his self and his body left Steve bemused.

Identity meaning is disrupted by its multiplicity. Discomfort in this case, then, derives from the momentary dislocation of the essentialist narrative of biology and nature: *if I am gay, then I am comfortable dressing gay, and therefore others will recognize that I am gay.* Expression of identity follows identity, which follows biology. Comfort follows from being a writerly rather than readerly text, although what is written may be highly context specific. The disruption of this "natural" flow of essentialistic discourse leads to a hyperperformativity of sexuality (the "I am gay" speech, the momentary power of the confessional, which is subsequently reinterpreted or ignored), which at once threatens exposure of identity itself as performative through the conflation of the binary of acting and being.[4]

Conclusion

Identity may be thought through on a number of levels—the academic (epistemological), the political (in terms of binaries), and the experiential (ontological). Different spaces of performativity afford subjects more or less critical distance from the performances of identity in which they engage, using a combination of political and ontological discourses. In this sense, work spaces, for example, may provide a vantage point from which to examine the disciplinary technologies of the self that are employed there, through the inevitable conflicts of discourse with ontology and perhaps the care of the self. However, rejection of hegemonic discourses may be expressed as individuality, rather than as the "other" social in which one is implicated. Subjects are likely to be less critical of such technologies that operate both on the "scene," reducing ontological contradictions and negative experiences of regulatory regimens to individual faults such as bitchiness, and least critical of all in the home, the perceived safe haven in which one can truly be "oneself."

Political discourses of sex, gender, and sexuality are ill-equipped to explain and examine the intricacies and the micropowerplays that take place in all spheres of the creation of the queer subject. Instead, these discourses set up false binaries that offer the subject little explanatory proficiency in negotiating the everyday technologies of the self. Thus, in order to negotiate a position, the subject often resorts to the cultural discourses of essen-

4. See Butler (1997) on "gay speech in the military." "I am gay" becomes a performative rather than a constative (descriptive) speech act.

tialism, prevalent in queer culture. The fixity of such positions, combined with the unworkability of standard political discourses, often seem to leave the subject disempowered, unable to explain or put into a cogent political context the ontological experiences that contradict these discourses.

Poststructuralist theories, especially those of performativity and of texts, provide much more satisfactory viewpoints from which to examine the minutiae of the everyday ontologies and self-presentations of identities (though such positions problematically leave little or no space for reflexivity or movement). Such theories are particularly suited to research conducted through video diaries, which highlight the visual presentation of selves. Rather than operating on some detached, abstract plane, poststructuralist theories are highly relevant and applicable to everyday identity ontologies.

Comfort for the diarists is ultimately produced in the harmony of self-explanations and self-presentations—the degree of fit between one's *explanation* of/for oneself and one's *expression* of that self, the inside and outside of one's body, the process of becoming a writerly text. Where some disjuncture appears between these discourses, discomfort is produced. Not having enough resemblance to one's "family" can for instance be disconcerting. Prevailing cultural and political discourses offer such harmonies only through fixity and conformity, in the Foucauldian sense through "knowing thyself"—the alignment of the self with situated discourses—even if these discourses are subcultural rather than hegemonic. This fixity or definition, as Butler points out, is always at the expense of exclusion or of an included but "haunted" subjectivity (by the ghost of the excluded "other" or "otherness"). What a poststructuralist politics provides is a shift from "knowing thyself" to "taking care of the self," the comfort of the alignment of the political to the body of the subject rather than vice versa.

But it is necessary to explore the notion of comfort further here. Why is *comfort* the term with which respondents choose to frame their identities? What is it that the diarists mean when they talk about comfort? We are used to the idea of physical comfort; some items include the term in their name—*chair*, for instance. There is also a developing notion of psychological comfort (standards of behavior, responsibilities, risks, temporal commitments, and so on that one feels comfortable with). But what is comfortable for one person may not be comfortable for another. So is comfort individual—an individualizing force? Richard Sennett gives us two accounts of comfort in his book *Flesh and Stone*. The first shows how comfort has become linked with individualism. "Comfortable ways to travel, like comfortable furniture and places to rest, began as aids for recovery from the bodily abuses marked by the sensations of fatigue. From its very origins, though, comfort had another trajectory, as comfort became synonymous with *individual* comfort" (1994, 339, emphasis added).

The development of comfortable chairs, carriages, and trains in the nineteenth century, Sennett argues, effectively erased the everyday sociability of public space. Tables placed outside cafes in nineteenth-century Paris "deprived political groups of their cover; the tables served customers watching the passing scene, rather than conspiring with one another [for political reform]" (345). These outside customers ceased to become social actors or political conspirators, becoming instead passive voyeurs or flaneurs. "On the terrace, the denizens of the cafe sat silently watching the crowd go by—they sat as individuals, each lost in his or her own thoughts . . . the people on the street now appearing as scenery, as spectacle" (346).

For Sennett then, "[c]omfort is of course a sensation easy to despise" (338). However, Sennett's argument at this point has much in common with criticism of new queer cultures, especially his discussion of cafés and of writings on queer café bars. The argument here is that the tables that spill onto the street prompt either a voyeuristic reaction from passing straights to which passive queers are subject or greater social acceptability through a loss of political dynamism from a toning down of queer behavior in order to be palatable to this voyeuristic public consumption (see Binnie 1995a). In order to move away from these oversimplistic accounts, I would like to employ Freud's (1914) concept of narcissism and especially the narcissistic gaze.

Unlike popular notions of narcissism, defined as self-love, Freud's position is not about desire for one's own reflection but for what the self would like to be, an idealized self. In another maneuver, one does not have simply desire for an object, the idealized self, but also an identification *with* the object—a desire to be it and to be desired by it. Thus, narcissistic desire is both desire *for* and desire *to be* one's idealized self (Lewis and Rolley 1997; Probyn 1995). If one maps this framework onto the social, queer subjects both desire the objects of their gaze (others whom they identify with an idealized version of themselves) and want to be their desired object, to be objectified by them. This scenario explains how shared cultural codes, of dress and adornment in particular, circulate in queer subcultures. That is not to say that all lesbians desire all lesbians (Probyn 1995), but that specific items of clothing and jewelry or haircuts or body modifications come to have currency in specific queer subcultures. It explains very neatly Jo's motivation for the purchase of her Adidas top. Finally, an important point to note here is that dressing up to go out on the scene is not simply a process of identifying oneself as a passive sexual object, but rather the double movement of having and being, creating an idealized self in the gaze of the other (object of one's desire). This explains one of the most fundamental and pleasurable *activities* of the scene: to look and be looked at (Bech 1997). As Lewis and Rolley conclude (in relation to fashion magazines, but I feel the argument holds in this context), "The importance of dress as a signifier of sexual identity, and of looking as a social, identifying and *sexualised* activity . . . coalesce[s] to provide a supplementary pleasure in the activity of consuming [queer culture]. As Walker . . . points out, 'looking like what you are' in terms of self-presentation is crucial for a recognisable [queer] identity and structurally central to the theorisation of marginal identities" (1997, 299). The comfort of identity is thus far from an individual or individualizing state within queer culture. Rather it is always social, though its *discourse* may sometimes carry the rhetoric of individualism.

There is a second part to Sennett's argument, however. He implies that comfort provides a kind of social detachment, a kind of separation from real connections with others. Being comfortable—as in comfortably off—implies a lack of necessity to worry about the world or one's position in it. Comfort is an easy, unthinking state. Perhaps, then, comfort means social and personal atrophy. It is not until one feels discomfort that one is able to move (or move on). Discomfort, or *displacement,* as Sennett calls it, dislodges social norms. It is often discomfort above all else that moves a queer subject to "come out," for instance. The discomfort of concealment is greater than that of disclosing one's sexuality, and this discomfort forces action. The comfort gained through many uncomfortable years of political struggle, the comfort of a revamped scene, the comfort of a more liberal state and of some protection from discrimination in the workplace have all produced a more comfortable (lesbian and gay) identity and politics. But perhaps comfort is to be feared because it is discomfort, displacement, disruption that move (queer) politics (and selves) forward into a more complex and less-exclusive or less-complacent place. As Sennett puts it, "Displacement thus becomes something quite different . . . from sheer movement. . . . Human displacements ought to jolt people into caring about one another, and where they are" (1994, 353).

4

Fragments for a Queer City

David Bell

> The city is a map of the hierarchy of desire, from the valorized to the stig-
> matized. It is divided into zones dictated by the way its citizens value or
> denigrate their needs. . . . In the city there are zones of commerce, of tran-
> sit, of residence. But some zones of the city cannot be so matter-of-fact
> about the purposes they serve. These are the sex zones—called red-light
> districts, combat zones, and gay ghettoes. . . . [T]here is no city in the
> world which does not have them. In part because of these zones, the city
> has become a sign of desire: promiscuity, perversity, prostitution, sex
> across the lines of age, gender, class, and race. (Califia 1994, 205)

In her landmark essay "The City of Desire: Its Anatomy and Destiny," Pat
Califia (1994) begins by sketch mapping an urban sexual fabric of "zones,"
borrowing a Chicago School language to think about how perverse pleasures are etched into the cityscape. In this chapter, I too want to think about
those sex zones and critically review some of the work that has been produced about them: to write a series of fragments for thinking the "queer
city." I also want to think about Califia's phrasing—that the city has "become a sign of desire"—by looking at attempts to theorize the special relationship between the urban and the sexually deviant.

It would appear that the sex zones of the contemporary Western city
have morphed into some interesting new configurations since Califia originally made her observations in the United States in the mid-1980s, and I
want to draw out some of the zones she doesn't discuss, as well as signal
the changes occurring in the "combat zones" and "gay ghettoes" she pin-
points (for an update on the city of desire, see Califia 1997). The city's sex
zones are much more diverse, much more complex, and much more a part

of the urban fabric than Califia suggests; her concentration on the informal economy or "hidden marketplace" of the sex zones to some extent writes out some of the spaces and places I want to consider; in fact, after discussing this issue with colleagues and friends, I found it quite difficult to think of *any* part of the urban fabric that isn't at least potentially an erogenous zone—from ATM foyers to libraries to office blocks, from night buses to scout huts to restaurants, and from construction sites to tupperware parties and football terraces—each site having its own distinctive erotics. Although significant contributions made to thinking about some of these spaces, many of these spaces remain uncontemplated—but not unused or unloved by urban sexual explorers.

I also want to argue that the character of the places Califia does discuss has in some cases changed quite remarkably. In particular, the constant trope of invisibility, which is so central to Califia's construction of urban desires, has faded, bringing a new and paradoxical sense of visibility to sexual "subcultures"—at once the angry visibility that fights erasure and the visibility that provokes voyeurism and censure, and calls for the protective veil of privacy. The chapter begins with the cityspace perhaps most closely implicated in these processes—the gay bar.

Gay Bars as Public Places

In an article published in *Landscape Research* in 1980, Barbara Weightman described American gay bars as "private places," marking a secret geography of unsigned, inconspicuous, anonymous backstreet bars and clubs in U.S. cities. Their internal geography, too, echoed with secrecy and seclusion: these places were not on any map, in tracts of seemingly abandoned industrial space on urban hinterlands (on the erotic possibilities of these urban ruins, see Jon Binnie's chapter in this volume). Califia's description of the "hidden market" of citysex carries similar emblems: "if one visits a sex zone at the wrong time of day, it may be unrecognizable. This type of marketplace is usually tolerated only between sunset and dawn" (1994, 206).[1] These places were forbidding, too—built around a solid insider/outsider dichotomy, such that the outsider would never, could never acciden-

---

1. Much more could be made of the diurnal patterning of citysex, of course—on the day and night activities, on the particular erotics of certain times (such as dusk, maybe, or the small hours).

tally stumble into this "twilight world," and only the insider, with all his or her secret knowledge, could search such places out, have the courage to go in, and find this hidden, forbidden world.

On my last visit to Manchester, England—a fast-growing "gay mecca" with a flourishing commercial scene—I was struck by the outdatedness of Weightman's and Califia's descriptions, for here is a sex zone extremely *visible*, a market not hidden but blatant; and here, too, we find the enactment of that contradiction I signaled above. In the window of one slick new gay bar was a notice that read:

This is a gay space. Please respect it.

There's obviously something very telling about such a notice, about the fact that such a statement requires enunciation, even in the heart of Manchester's self-styled Gay Village. This, then, is the paradox of queer visibility in commerical urban space—one of the perils of the pink economy. As Jenny Ryan and Hilary Fitzpatrick write in their account of the ambivalence arising out of the transformations of the Gay Village from " 'marginal,' backstreet, seedy venues to . . . new, liminal, public spaces, . . .[b]ecause it is both 'trendy' and 'gay,' the space it provides makes visible the potential tensions between different groups of urban consumers" (1996, 176–77). Their day's diary of the pseudonymed "Otto's Bar" in the Village pieces together a sequence of time geographies, each with its own forms of sexualization, from the city center business lunch crowd to the afternoon tea set and the evening's preclub cruisers. As Jon Binnie suggested to me, perhaps a better subtitle for this section would be "Gay Bars as Straight Places," for the complex and ambiguous construction and performance of sexual identities is at the heart of the tensions Ryan and Fitzpatrick describe in what have sometimes become seen as "mixed spaces." Visibility, then, seems for some people to incur a reliquishing of control (although Ryan and Fitzpatrick describe the management of inclusion and exclusion through changing door-policy regimes as a way of addressing the shifting needs of the day's clienteles) and the opening up of "gay space" to (straight) colonization. As with the ambivalence of "queer inclusivity" (with "queer hetero" being seen by some folk as the most contradiction-riven identity; see Bell and Valentine 1995a), the spatial outcomes of slick marketing and a visible city-center location (and of

course, great food, drink, and music) clearly mark these gay bars as paradoxical space.

A Lover's Disco

In the related (but in some ways quite distinct) world of gay discos and
clubs, similar (and also very different) imperatives are at work.[2] Although
in the United Kingdom the rise of the Ecstasy-based "rave" culture
through the 1980s and 1990s cemented a "mixed" scene for clubbing,
where the straight/gay (and male/female, black/white, etc.) distinction
was displaced by the "Summer of Love" and its fabled inclusiveness, gay
club culture has also had to respond to some incredibly pressing reconfigurations. The impact of HIV and AIDS is paramount because the sexualized performance of clubbing has inevitably been reshaped by the
epidemic's dance floor (and backroom) epicenters. Here again, the "no sex,
just love" feel of Ecstasy has had a substantial effect, but also important, as
Gregory Bredbeck writes, is contemporary gay disco as a historicized enactment of gay identity and identification—a post-Stonewall (and post-
AIDS) reappropriation of the (forbidden) pleasures of dancing to disco as
an interpellative or performative project of the self. As Bredbeck is careful
to point out, disco has embedded within it all the "junctions and disjunc-
tions between gay men and lesbians and between the disparate attitudes
towards eroticism and politics" (1996, 80) that still exist, even within the
problematic inclusiveness of the queer generation. But he is also keen to
celebrate disco's place in gay culture, while assessing its changing (and un-
changing) roles (see also Currid 1995; Dyer 1992).

It's interesting that in a section of his essay called "Disco in Time: The
History Mix," Bredbeck quotes from the 1973 *Joy of Gay Sex,* where Edmund White wrote the following about gay discos: "Gone are the days of
the sleazy hideaway bars buried in basements and as hard to enter as
speakeasies. Now hundreds of gays troop into big, spacious, luxurious discos where the dancing, the sounds, the lights and the company are great. In
fact, the main problem the gay discos face is how to keep straights from

2. The title of this section pays homage to Elspeth Probyn's comment (made I can't remember where) that she always mischievously misreads the title of Roland Barthes's *A
Lover's Discourse* as *A Lover's Disco.*

moving in and elbowing out the original gay clientele" (Silverstein and White 1973, 83, quoted in Bredbeck 1996, 81). So twenty years before Ryan and Fitzpatrick's mapping of the spatial tensions of "Otto's Bar," White describes exactly the same problematique: gay discos as public (and therefore potentially straight) places. Henning Bech notes, with a hint of lament, that "heterosexuals eventually got their discos" (1997, 123). Bech's description of the special place of the disco in modern gay life is, in fact, particularly campy (in the way sociology can sometimes be camp) and engaging; anyone who can write "You strike up a pose when at the disco . . . you act, if you have succeeded in learning it, that you are a sex object dancing" *cannot* be wholly serious.[3] He ends (and I will end) on a crescendo, a disco whirl (cue music and lights): "it is a space of energy, *high-energy*, a space for discharging and recharging, for motoric activity. . . . The energy of light and sound fuses with the physical energy of those present. Sexual energy?— not really, or kind of. *Sensual* energy, rather: emotions turn into energy, pure energy, stylized energy" (Bech 1997, 123, emphasis in original).

Sexing the Public

More often than to the semipublic commercial spaces through which I have just danced, the focus of work on citysex has turned to a variety of urban public spaces and has observed, recorded, and discussed the erotic practices of so-called public sex. From the American urban sociology tradition that brought us Humphries's controversial *Tearoom Trade* (1970) and an associated raft of troublesome ethnographic accounts, a story has evolved of casual sex in urban public spaces, recounted through the distanced, objective eyes of the Researcher [4]—although Joseph Styles's (1979) uncharacteristically naked account of his increasing immersion into gay bathhouse culture never fails to entertain me, with its mix of sociological distancing and sexual intimacy. (As Bech puts it, in these accounts "science turns into pornography" [1997, 113].)

Of course, as Les Moran (1996) once said, the first ethnographers of public sex (apart from the participants themselves)—and the producers of the first maps of these erogenous zones—were the police, with plain-

3. On camp and antiseriousness in the academy, see Bell 1995b, Binnie 1995b, Travers 1993.

4. On geography's troubled and troubling objectivity in this sense, see Binnie 1997a.

clothes officers on entrapment operations painstakingly recording "offenses" in public toilets or at after-dark parks (see also Moore 1995 on cruising grounds or "beats" in Australia).[5] In every city's collection of "random nooks" (Bech 1997, 111), such zones, such spaces for meetings (and more), may evolve:

> The city is there. Instead of trying to get away from it, you can enter it; instead of closing your eyes to it, you can open them, and see what comes of it. The brief contacts and one-off meetings are one way of tackling the reality of the city: the fact that you are among strangers; that there are lots of them and that there are constantly new ones; that you yourself are exposed surface and hidden interior, clandestine receiver and live signal; that the mixture of proximity and distance, surface and depth, crowd and loneliness is at once attractive and alarming. The city lays down needs. (Bech 1997, 112)

There are, of course, many similar (and familiar) arguments about the "privacy" of public places and of public sex (Bell 1995a; Edelman 1994; Moran 1996; Woodhead 1995)—about the simultaneous coexistence of the public and the private in the same space: a public toilet is still a public toilet even if it is also a cottage or tearoom. In fact, as Moran points out, Britain's most significant piece of legislation targeting homosexuals, the 1967 Sexual Offences Act, specifically addressed this problem: "An act which would otherwise be treated for the purposes of this Act as private shall not be so treated if done (a) when more than two persons take part or are present; or (b) in a lavatory to which the public have or are permitted to have access, whether on payment or otherwise" (1996, 142). Although the first clause has its own dangerous resonances (to which we shall turn later), the specifying of public toilets *as public* is our principal concern here,

---

5. Police records of undercover entrapment encounters with public sex are often so coyly worded that academics (myself included) cannot resist quoting them; see, for example, Moran, citing a report of cottaging in London in 1933: "After a few minutes the prisoner made a half-turn towards me, stretched out his left arm and placed his left hand on my person and commenced rubbing it" (1996, 147); and Moore on some interrupted beach frolics in Queensland in 1870: "With my right hand I shoved down between the privates of the prisoner Boyd and the fundament of the prisoner Reily. I then found the prisoner Boyd's penis which was quite rigid and inserted in the prisoner Reily's fundament. The prisoner Boyd's penis was quite greasy and wet" (1995, 332). To paraphrase Bech (1997), *policing becomes pornography.*

for law has a duty to police public space and, with the specific imperatives of the clause quoted above, to deny privacy (including sexual privacy) therein. Hence, the most concentrated policing activities around homosexuality in the United Kingdom (and elsewhere) center on public toilets doubling as cottages: "the cottage becomes a space for the unclothed and the plain-clothed" (Woodhead 1995, 239).

Although public toilets offer the most concentrated realization of this public-private, liberation-regulation paradox, many other "random nooks" in the cityscape have a similar role to play, producing a "finely calibrated sexual map of the city" (Chauncey 1996, 249). Indeed, this map changes constantly, as increased hostile attention at one site leads to its desertification, while new windows of opportunity open up elsewhere. The tactics of cruising are particularly malleable and opportunist—adapting to the range of situations present—and anything from the "gay fiction" section of the local bookstore to a seemingly anonymous parking lot or the aisles of a supermarket can become part of the cruiser's erotic topography.[6] Of course, there need be no recognizable or informally designated site or zone—as work on the general erotic potential of the city streets attests (e.g., Bech 1997; Bell and Binnie 1998; Chauncey 1996; Munt 1995). George Chauncey's historical geography of New York's gay street life makes precisely this point: "gay men [in the 1920s and 1930s] devised a variety of tactics that allowed them to move freely about the city, to appropriate for themselves spaces that were not marked as gay, and to construct a gay city in the midst of, yet invisible to, the dominant city" (1996, 225). The policing of male-male public sex, Chauncey argues, needs contextualizing as part of a bourgeois reordering of public (and private) space, in common with the regulation of other (e.g., working-class) street cultures and activities—a hegemonic project that failed because of the diverse and complex acts and identities inhabiting (and resisting in) that space, which to some extent survived because of their invisibility to the "dominant city."

Central to understanding the particular erotics of the street, of course,

6. A student of mine, writing an essay on the city and sexual outlawry, made this point in connection with certain shelves of her local branch of Waterstone's, a British book-selling chain. And, of course, Armistead Maupin immortalized supermarket cruising in his *Tales of the City* series; interestingly, at least one British supermaket chain has sought to capitalize on its function as unofficial dating agency, running "singles nights," with heart-shaped pizza and piped romantic music (Bell and Valentine 1997), and the Virgin chain of record stores holds "gay nights."

are theories of flâneurie and of the gaze. Although there have been intense critiques of both of these practices, productive accounts have also emerged, which have managed to overstep or sidestep some of the stumbling blocks (such as the flâneur's perceived masculinism/heterosexism). Sally Munt's (1995) famous and evocative essay on the lesbian flâneur, for example, recuperates the figure of the "urban stroller" within an erotics of women looking and being looked at by women out on the city streets, and reads the lesbian flâneur's presence in literary representations of New York dykelife. And Bech's discussion of the gaze accords it centrality for both homosexual identity and the erotic possibilities of the urban:

> The gaze belongs to the city. Only when there is mutual strangeness does it exist; and the city supplies strangers galore. In the country, there is no gaze, but instead an all-embracing visibility.... [In the city] everyone walks down the street, and *everyone* is free to look at everyone.... The homosexual, then, develops the gaze. Conversely, it may be that the gaze develops the homosexual: another man's surface captivating one's glance, another man's gaze meeting one's own and arousing interest. Whatever the case, it is impossible to be homosexual without having a gaze. (1997, 108)

There are, of course, easily spotted faults with Bech's generalizations—in the prioritization of vision as opposed to tactility and in the neglect of the fact that the gaze doesn't operate only with gays, but has an equal role to play in heterosexual and bisexual urban life—but that's not really the point: his stress on the gaze in the constitution of homosexuality itself marks the streets as potentially *the* most erotic of urban erogenous zones.

Passing is another important dimension to the queer use of sidewalks. As has been argued elsewhere, the subtleties of the gaze and the codings of homosexual performance mean that the adoption of seemingly nonhomosexual identities in public space can offer the transgressive pleasures of passing—as well, perhaps, as some modicum of safe invisibility from the homophobic gaze (Bell et al. 1994). Although passing, too, is not unproblematic, it should be registered as another fragment for the queer city. Indeed, as Chauncey's (1996) account suggests, this outsider-invisible, insider-visible ordering of queer space has always been an important component of homosexual public culture; the current manifestations—gay male hypermasculine and lesbian hyperfeminine identities—merely mark an added transgressive take on the long history of this ambivalent existence of two simultaneous worlds on the city's streets.

In an interesting further twist, we should also record activist strategies that work to explode the heteronormativity of public space through radical eruptions of queer visibility (Bell and Valentine 1995d; Davis 1995; Geltmaker 1992). As part of an evolving set of activist strategies associated with both queer politics and AIDS politics, these tactics work to undermine both assumptions about the heterosexuality of public space and public ritual, and the concomitant silencing and invisibilizing of sexual dissidence. Actions such as kiss-ins, queer nights out, wink-ins, and queer weddings represent an "embodied geography of raging activism" (Bell and Valentine 1995d, 153), with rallying cries such as "Whose fucking streets? *Our* fucking streets!" raising questions about what (and who) can be *public* in public space. As the flip side to passing, then, the theatrical spectacle of queer visibility takes to the streets with considerable sex-political charge: enraged or aroused, public or private,[7] the place of the streets in urban queer culture could not be more central or so multidimensional.

Sodomy in Suburbia

> I could *never* live in the suburbs. (Golding 1997)

If the streets are ambivalently public, then the domestic(ated) space of suburbia stands in interesting contrast. Although the role of (especially) gay men in the gentrifying revival of metropolitan living has been very well rehearsed (see, for example, Knopp 1990b) and the image of the "gay ghetto" has been cemented in the (gay and straight) imaginary, comparatively little attention has been given to the sexual symbolics of the suburban (other than to consider a set of masculine-feminine codings; see Bondi 1992). The English suburb, however, has a peculiar place in the perverse geography of the city: it has been mythologized as the site of illicit pleasures (wife swapping, sex parties) always hidden behind net curtains, of sin clothed in respectability and mundanity (Hunt 1998). As explored in Hanif Kureshi's

---

7. This description does not imply that rage and arousal are always separate, or that rage is public, whereas arousal is private. The enrage/arouse couplet comes from a Gay Men Fighting AIDS (GMFA) publicity campaign in London that combined porn images with AIDS statistics.

(1990) *The Buddha of Suburbia,* for example, the suburban always has a saucy or sleazy underbelly (see also Oswell 1996, n.d.). As David Oswell puts it, "behind the closed net curtains a whole set of debauched and sinister activities are allowed to take place" (n.d., 13); or, as John Hartley disapprovingly writes, suburbia is "also the site of sexual perversity, domestic violence, incest and anorexia" (1997, 185).

Oswell argues that queer—as a metropolitan movement—is defined against the ordinary, for which he reads the suburban (Califia makes a similar point about the mutual constitution of "sex zones" and "ostensibly safe residential enclaves designated for child rearing and monogamous marriage" [1994, 206]). But, as Oswell then suggests in relation to *The Buddha of Suburbia* and to David Lean's film *Brief Encounter,* the suburban itself is ripe for a certain kind of eroticization: "the sense of restraint, of discreteness and of gentility exhibited . . . cannot simply be typified as an 'English' repression of desire. On the contrary, desire is produced out of these refined morals and manners: a kind of sexual etiquette of teatime foreplay" (n.d., 13). It might be argued here that this is a distinct fetishization of English suburbia; and, in fact, the suburb has many subtley different metanymic functions in other settings. In England, it chimes with middle-class "respectability," semidetatched residential developments, male commuters and their dometicated families, and so on. Other meanings of the suburban might produce very different forms of sexualization (such as lower-class, "white trash" neighborhoods in the United States).

Accounts like Oswell's are suprisingly rare in the academy; in fact, as John Hartley says, "[s]cholars scarcely venture into suburbia except to pathologize it" (1997, 186). He goes on to write of straight, Australian suburbs: "sexy they ain't (yet), despite the fact that this is where homes are traditionally set up by couples at the start of their sexually active careers, where children are begotten and where teenagers first learn about sex, in short where sex actually happens" (1997, 208).

The few studies of "gay suburbia" that have thus far appeared have not particularly reflected Oswell's erotics of the 'burbs either, instead supporting Hartley's notion of a desexed (or presexed) suburbia and describing a curious combination of, on the one hand, a "refreshingly open and relaxed" attitude toward homosexuality and, on the other, "threatening and repressive" tendencies among straight suburbanites (Lynch 1992, 168). Certainly, without access in the suburbs to the same diversity of both commercial and informal gay spaces, the "nonghetto gays" in Fredrick Lynch's sample tended to rely on nearby cities for much of their contact with "gay life." Signs of a "suburban sensibility," too, were detected among Lynch's male respondents (which is, in part, *not* related to sexuality but rather to place), as well as signs of the evolution of a semidistinct suburban gay culture (assimilationist, sexually restrained, or at least discrete, in short *respectable*)—significantly, with no hint of the behind-net-curtains debauchery that Oswell suggests in his work. Lynch points out that "Most of those formally interviewed were politely verbal in social settings. They were able and unafraid of ordinary give-and-take dialogue and banter. Serious conversation about politics or culture was generally avoided. Restrained hugs and kisses were used in exchanging greetings. Other than that, there was little or no toleration of effeminate behavior" (1992, 191). Of course, Lynch's sample is of a very specific subset of *suburban homosexuals* (the term he used in order not to alienate those scared of terms such as *gay*), so perhaps it isn't surprising that he finds no signs of sex-radical promiscuity, orgies, and dungeons hidden in suburban semis.[8]

As a final brief encounter with the erotics of the suburban, I want to mention my favorite category in the personal ads of British gay freesheet *Boyz:* among more familiar columns for bootboys, rubber lovers, watersports fans, and so on is a section called "City Gents." Making a fetish of the outwardly "respectable" business commuter seems to me a perfect summing up of sexy suburbia (see also Hallam 1993).

8. The media, of course, love such scandalous suburban stories, and there are periodic flourishes during which assorted forms of debauchery are exposed, usually frivolously (and titillatingly)—one British example being tabloid stories of the "Bi-Sex Boom" (Eadie 1992). More seriously, the "Operation Spanner" male-male sadomasochism case in the United Kingdom (together with subsequent operations, such as the raid on a house party in Hoylandswaine, Yorkshire) might conceivably be read as part of that tradition, although the consequences for those individuals convicted certainly were not frivolous (see Moran 1995; Stanley 1993). The SM scene, certainly in Britain, in fact seems a peculiarly suburban phenomenon in some ways; the photographs in Polhemus and Randall's (1994) *Rituals of Love,* for example, often appear irrevocably suburban (see "Master Keith" on page 77, Claire and Brian on 117). This point is also parodied in David Shenton's cartoons "Suburban Aboriginals," which mock the title of the famous SM manual *Urban Aboriginals* (Mains 1984). And I've just noticed that my informal shorthand notes for this chapter say "Sub—dom," reminding myself that the space of the suburb is always coded as domestic; funny that it brings to mind another fetish of the suburban-domestic: sub(ordination)-dom(ination), with its connotations of kinky dominatrices and masochistic businessmen doing the dusting for kicks.

Home as Pleasure Zone

The suburb is, as has already been said, most often seen as domestic space.[9] The streets of suburbia are not the streets cruised in my earlier discussion of flâneurie and gay gazing; the suburb is a home place, with its emphasis on homely pursuits (hence its frequent feminization). But that is also a key part of its eroticization—rude things going on behind net curtains, in living rooms and bedrooms rather than in backrooms, in avenues rather than in alleyways. So, in this section, I want to think about the home—that most private of private spaces—and, in particular, to look at ways in which domestic privacy becomes public (some of these ideas are rehearsed in Bell 1995a).

Work on queer homemaking has tended largely to focus on either metropolitan gentrification (Knopp 1990a, 1990b; Rothenberg 1995) or the complexities of identity negotiation in domestic space (Johnston and Valentine, 1995). As Johnston and Valentine tease out, the meanings of the lesbian home (parental home, site of abuse, haven from homophobia, and so on) are "numerous and beset with contradictions" (1995, 112). Their essay includes an interesting discussion about privacy and about the complex ways in which the need for privacy is negotiated and contested through the space of the home; as they say, the home is "not necessarily a place of privacy" (1995, 112). It is precisely this ambivalent relation between the domestic and the private that I want to stay with a little while here.

Privacy is something enshrined for citizens as a right within law, yet its definition is somewhat flexible and often intangible. Judith Squires (1994) has written eloquently on the matter of privacy as a constitutional underpinning of "civilized society" and on the erosion (or redefinition) of the private by surveillance and information technologies. If privacy is to be thought of as "power over the space which surrounds one" (1994, 390) and, equally crucially, as "control over one's body" (399), then the relation of the domestic to the private in the context of the queer city must obviously be explored.[10]

---

9. The title of this section is adapted from the fabulous slogan of interior design and style bible *Elle Decoration*, "Make your home a pleasure zone."

10. Squires (1994) suggests it may be necessary to uncouple our sense of privacy from the "private sphere" because the penetration of surveillance and information technologies into that sphere forces on us a redefinition of *where* privacy can be found.

In the case of "unlawful" sex, the 1967 Sexual Offences Act in the United Kingdom, already quoted, tried to straddle a delicate line between the toleration and respect of privacy (even queer privacy) and the specific limiting of what constitutes the private. It thus recognized a very circumscribed form of the private in the case of male-male sex: two (and no more) men, both over the age of consent, out of sight and earshot of anyone else, and in private space (for which read the home—if at all possible, in fact, read the bedroom), not doing anything too perverse; using no props, toys, or aids (which can, under some circumstances, be classified as obscene materials—not just whips or dildos, but leather jackets and jeans); leaving no material trace (no photos, no videos—which too can be classed as obscene, even if they're not for public circulation); and so on (Bell 1995a). The domestic space of the home, then, is only precariously private (and not only for sexual deviants: the British government is currently working out a new Police Bill, which will give law enforcement unbridled access to the homes and offices of "suspected criminals" and new powers to use surveillance equipment in domestic space—intense civil liberties protests notwithstanding). As Mark Wigley writes, "Privacy is a public construction" (1992, 377), a construction to which not everyone has equal rights.

The home, then, should perhaps fall into the category of *combat zones* to which Califia alludes, for it is a site of many forms of battle—most notably over the right to privacy in a broader sense than that defined by law. To adapt the point Hartley makes with reference to suburbia, the home is the site for lots of sex, even if it hasn't figured so centrally in discourses of sexual liberation. And, as with the suburbs again, the domestic produces its own forms of sexualization—whether it's playboy-bachelor pads (Cohan 1996) or housework fetishists; as the site of so much sex, then, the home can (indeed should) figure as sexy, kinky, queer.

Motion and Emotion

In recent discourses of the contemporary city, increasing emphasis is being placed not on fixed locations such as the home, but on tropes of movement and flow. The previous discussion of the city streets similarly stressed the erotics of the body in motion—of fleeting moments of interaction and the flicker of images. Henning Bech has this to say about one particular site of mobile erotics:

What is it about railway stations that draws the homosexual? First and foremost, that they *concentrate* the city. All the elements are there, compacted and condensed within a delimited space: the crowd, the constant flux of new people, the mutual strangeness and indifference; the feeling of motion, options, sexual excitement, potential danger and surveillance; the possibilities for moving and following, for using gaze, sending signals, disappearing in the crowd, etc. . . . The special thing about the station is that it is also a *travel space,* a place for departures and arrivals. Hence additional moods that vibrate with those of the homosexual: of breaking up, of something fluid, less complete and clear-cut, of chronic transit from one point of life to another. And yearnings, dreams, of going away, of experiences and adventures, of another country. (1997, 159)

In this remarkably evocative passage, Bech captures the sexualization of movement, both literal and metaphorical, found in that concentration of city life that is the railway station—an image that has found its way into many popular cultural representations of contemporary queer life (one that springs to mind is Derek Jarman's backdrop movie footage for the Pet Shop Boys' lamenting "King's Cross," featured on his video collection *Projections*). There's a strong hint of melancholy, too, in both Jarman's footage and Bech's description—of yearnings and chronic transit: displacement, maybe, or restlessness or dispossession. Echoing Bech's description, Van Gelder and Brandt write of lesbian and gay tourists, "the outside perspective of the traveler is second skin to us" (1992, xiii).

Transport geography is, of course, part of the discipline that hasn't yet stopped to consider sexuality, though there is obviously need for intervention, to consider how transport mobilizes queer identity, whether through the experience of travel itself; through the functioning of crossroads, intersections, and terminals as erogenous zones (on highway rest areas, truck stops, and so on, see Corzine and Kirby 1977; Lieshout 1995; Ponte 1974; Troiden 1974); or through the erotic uses of modes of transport themselves. I have heard anecdotally about elaborate systems of "car cruising" in some cities, and Jerry Lee Kramer's (1995) fine account of rural gay life describes the key function of the car in opening up opportunities for country boys (and girls) to find companionship and sex. Chauncey (1996), too, notes the washrooms on New York's subway system (and, indeed, the subway cars themselves) as a vital part in the erotic topography of the city during the period he discusses.

Of course, travel is, as Bech notes, also about dreaming, having adventures, and finding (or hoping to find) "another country." And gay tourist practices clearly work to fulfil that yearning for other places, contributing to the formation of one form of transnational queer culture (Bell and Binnie 1996). Certain cities thus become points on a global map of queer sex zones—sites of pilgrimage, of a paradoxical sense of "coming home." This is, however, only one such "perverscape," to borrow the suffix of Arjun Appadurai's (1990) discussion of disjunctive global flows. Along with tourists, we must also remember migrants, exiles, and refugees, whose patterns and motives for movement—and whose reception by "host" cultures—can be markedly different (Binnie 1997a). The sexual politics of mobility, then, must always be seen as nonisomorphic, unpredicatable lines of flight, made of both choices and constraints, freedom and oppression, and mapping metropolitan spaces with both positive and negative valencies.

Thinking of the city as a "space of flows" also immediately calls to mind cyberspace because the disembedding effects of new communications technologies have been widely cited as offering opportunities for reconfigurations of identity and (virtual) community in what Bill Mitchell (1995) calls the "city of bits." The particular enabling features of cyberspace for identity and community formation are already in place to some extent in the more technologically humble but absolutely central communications infrastructure of personal ads run through the gay press (especially in the United Kingdom, the freesheets such as *Boyz* or *The Pink Paper*) and in the telephone help lines, chat lines, and sex lines (Brown 1995). In effect, queer cyberspace does little more than to extend these facilities, broadening their reach to the global (in theory, at least). The more hyped or profound impacts of cyberspace aside, its primary roles remain information, entertainment (including erotic entertainment), interpersonal contact, identity play, and (potentially at least) community building; the impacts of these roles on the urban could be considered as the construction of a "queer city of bits" (or perhaps a "city of queer bits"?), a new form of social space that is placeless in the conventional sense, but that offers many of the celebrated opportunities of the urban collected in virtual fragments.

Queer Country

Bech's evocation of travel as the search for another country and the previous discussion of cyberspace and its cousins take us on a digression away from the urban and toward the rural because it has recently been remarked that the overwhelming concentration on sex zones in the city has been at the cost of neglecting the countryside as an erotic resource and as a place where queer cultures (often very distinct from their metropolitan counterparts) if not thrive then certainly survive (Bell and Valentine 1995c; Kramer 1995). Of course, the city and the country exist in tension, and this is no less true for sexual dissidents; Kath Weston (1995) records the pull of metropolitan queer life on lesbians and gay men born and raised in the countryside in what she terms the "Great Gay Migration" in the United States—a migration that continues to this day. In my own work with Gill Valentine on "queer country," we found a more complex contemporary pattern of both permanent and temporary movements to and from rural areas, reflecting at least in part the contradictory imagining of both country and city (Bell and Valentine 1995c). For lesbian feminists, the rural may offer the best site to escape the patriarchal and heteronormative strictures embodied in the urban fabric; add to this contemporary spiritual and ecological trends in some quarters of queer culture, plus a general societal orientation toward forms of rural recreation and pleasure, and the country begins to exert a powerful pull on some people, whereas for others (perhaps especially those born and raised in villages and small towns) it remains insular, small-minded, close-knit, and overbearingly, impossibly heterosexist (Kramer 1995).

As an imaginitive resource, too, the wilderness exerts a powerful force as a place unfettered by the constraining rules of "civilization"—an Arcadia for free sexual play, for being one with nature rather than (as homosexuality became pathologized by science) forever being "against nature" (Fone 1983). With surges of urbanization reshaping the social landscape, the nostalgic, romantic appeal of Edenic innocence became fully felt; Bech writes that "[t]he 'countryside' which formed the setting of the fictitious world in which homosexuality could be consummated was often precisely the country of the city, projected beyond the city" (1997, 149). It must be recorded here, then, as a fragment for the queer city, that the city exists hand in hand with the country, each making and remaking the other.

Thinking the Queer City: Unforeseen Games

> From the erogenous zones emerge ideas. (Lefort 1996)

The preceding is not intended as a comprehensive catalog or map of the sex zones of the contemporary city; it has been written, rather, as a series of snapshots and suggestions to add to the process of theorizing the links between the urban and sexual dissidence. There are obviously missing pieces and links, some of which are well attended to elsewhere (in Jon Binnie's work on ruins in chapter 5, for example). The time has come, however, to assess what we might learn from our psychogeographical journey through the queer city.

In the title of an essay published in 1980, Dolores Hayden posed a powerful question: "What would a non-sexist city be like?" At base, I think I have been asking a very similar question here: *What would a queer city be like?* And thus far our answer is to be found by collecting together the fragments presented above. But part of the answer is to be found elsewhere, perhaps in the imaginative theorizing of the experience of the city, in the mapping of " 'vernacular' erotic geographies" (Pfohl 1993, 192). That's partly why I have kept a close eye on Henning Bech's *When Men Meet:* it offers considerable insight into "the homosexual form of existence," as he rather stiffly calls it (1997, 84–159). Bech plainly says, "the city is the social world proper of the homosexual, his life space"; in his discussion of the gaze, of meetings, of stagings and signals, railway stations and discos, he paints a clear and candid picture of the city's role in the production of the homosexual, its "omnipresent, diffuse sexualization" (1997, 118). Although there have been criticisms of Bech's supposed tendency to oversimplify (see, for example, Knopp 1995), his approach makes fertile connections with other currents of urban thinking we might draw on here. One such connection I would like to make is with the work of the Situationist International.

Reading a recent reprint of Constant's "A Different City for a Different Life" (1997, originally published 1959), I was struck by its resonances as a potential manifesto for the queer city. "We require adventure," Constant wrote. "We intend to break the laws that prevent the development of meaningful activities in life and culture" (1997, 109). His radical vision unfolds thus: "The future cities we envisage will offer an unusual variety of sensations . . . and unforeseen games will become possible through the inventive use of material conditions" (111). In another key Situationist tract, Ivan Chtcheglov suggested, "the districts of the city could correspond to the whole spectrum of diverse feelings that one encounters *by chance* in everyday life" (1981, 4, originally published 1953), building on the Situationists' notion of the *dérive* or drift—a kind of unconstrained wandering around urban public space at the whim of one's desires (see Debord 1981, originally published 1958). The *dérive* is suggestive of a more embodied, engaged, immersed experiencing of urban street life than the flâneur's sometimes cold, objectifying detachment—the kind of sensuous geography memorably found in Alphonso Lingis's epic *Foreign Bodies* (see also Bell 1996 and Binnie in this volume):

> It happens that in the night and the long loneliness of an alien city the torments of one's flesh move one to respond to a chance encounter. One exchanges only first names, and if the other finds my foreign name difficult to pronounce, I change it. This incomprehended and destitute stranger before me offers her or his body, abyss of unmarked wounds and dark exhilarations, in an imperative assignation. I denude myself and give myself over to the strange passions of a stranger; we part without compensation or exaction. (1994, 222–23)

Lingis's poetic description of this libidinal economy enacted on strange streets brings together Bech's "homosexual form of existence" (though Lingis suggests a more polymorphous, fluid sexuality) with the Situationists' chance encounters and ludic urbanity: an embodied interaction with the living, sexy city. More than Califia's regimented designation of erogenous zones (which maybe we could read into Chtcheglov's "mood-districts" [1981]), the city is an unending flow of possibilities (or *situations,* to use the Situationists' terminology)—an erotic topography that changes with one's moods and fantasies. (Constant proposed flexible cityscapes responsive to citizens' changing collective life patterns; Chtcheglov called architecture the "simplest means of . . . engendering dreams" [1981, 2], but more than architecture, the queer city can be seen as an embodied experience of sexualized space and place, perhaps.)

Of course, one could easily question the material realities, the issues of power and inequality that constellate around such a dreamscape of urban erotics, but that's not really my point here. I'm interested in thinking these fragments as utopian moments, as pleasure zones, as fantasy; interested in the "creative and wild possibilities" of the city, to use Sue Golding's (1993b, 217) delicious phrase. Golding's kinky threesome of essays (1993a, 1993b, 1993c) are among my favorites for thinking the city as a space of free (erotic) play. When she writes that "these words: dom, Master, bottom, whore-fem, butch, Daddy-boy, cruising, play, play-mate, and so on, have their place. . . . They make an impossible place take place. They describe, circumscribe, inscribe a spectacular space, a spectacle of space" (1993c, 80), she is thinking the queer city in the ways I'm hoping to capture it here: it is to be found in the " 'elsewhere' of decadent urban life" (88). Echoing Constant's phrase, she says, "We are the thieves who play with and against the Law . . . [a]nd in so doing, create, disrupt, invent, duplicate, a 'homeland' identity" (1993a, 26), describing a "very raw and fluid public space" (1993b, 216) created out of transgression and resistance.

The queer city, then, is more than the sum of its parts; the city is, to remember Califia, a "sign of desire" in itself, a place of "creative and wild possibilities," "of unforeseen games," whether they are found in railway stations or suburban semis, in bookshops or sex shops, on the dance floor or the shop floor, on the streets or between the sheets.

5

The Erotic Possibilities of the City

Jon Binnie

*Stories about places are makeshift things. They are composed of the world's de-
bris. . . . Within the structured space of the text, they thus produce anti-texts, effects of dissimulation and escape, possibilities of moving into other landscapes,
like cellars and bushes. . . . The dispersion of stories points to the dispersion of
the memorable as well. And in fact memory is a sort of anti-museum: it is not lo-
calizable. Fragments of it come out in legends.*—Michel de Certeau, *The Practice of Everyday Life*

The relationship between bodies and buildings, desires and the material
fabric of the city has begun to be explored in a burgeoning literature within
architectural theory (e.g., Colomina 1992; Perez-Gomez 1994; Ruedi, Wigglesworth, and McCorquodale 1996; and Vidler 1992). Beyond the walls of
the academy, the experimental novelist Iain Sinclair has poetically traced
the contours of the flows of desires, memories, and connections between
buildings and places in pasts and presents of (East) London (Sinclair 1991,
1997). Perhaps it is only in the astonishing creativity of Sinclair's books—
fictional, but always resisting the distinction between reality and fantasy—
that we can really explore the limits of representing desire in the city
beyond the constraints of academic discourse. Elsewhere I have discussed
the materialization of sexual desire by assessing the role of the *visual* in creating queer space (Binnie 1995a), arguing that the visual has been privileged in debates on the gendered and sexualized nature of urban space.
However, in this chapter, I wish to widen the discussion to consider embodiment more generally. How may we construct a *tactile,* embodied geography of the city, when intimacy and body fluids have become

103

synonymous with death in the time of AIDS? Elsewhere I have also argued that gay male sadomasochistic (SM) culture has expanded the limits of erotic possibility (Binnie 1997), suggesting that sadomasochists tend to regard themselves as pioneers of sexual experimentation and pleasure, exploring the limits and boundaries of sexual desire. In this chapter, I wish to bring these two arguments together; I explore the erotic possibilities and real physical dangers embodied in urban spaces of sexual danger—ruined churches, wastelands, derelict sites—spaces where fantasies are lived out. I argue that SM culture is also expanding the boundaries of consciousness and the embodiment of the urban experience.

A number of authors have argued that gay men have been pioneers in the economic restructuring of the North American city. According to Castells and to Knopp, gay men have played a key role in the gentrification process (Castells 1983; Knopp 1987, 1990a, 1990b, 1995). However, these economic-based analyses have failed to examine where desire, sex, and pleasure figure in the reimagineering and revalorization of these urban spaces. In the urban realm, gay men have been commonly associated with the places "we don't talk about"—what Califia terms the "sex zones" of the city. However, as I argue later, gay consumption spaces have become a dynamic force in the enterprise culture of a number of British cities, which has led to sexual cultures that are marginal to and within gay male culture—specifically lesbian cultures, SM cultures, and "public-sex" cultures—and that are becoming more marginal than ever before. So whereas cappucino culture thrives, the more overtly sexual, threatening, and queer have been pushed out. Queers are associated with the discarded, the derelict—the ruins of the urban landscape.

In homophobic discourse, gay men have been commonly represented as the "waste of modernity"—as the Other (Dellamora 1990). Nonproductive sexualities have been seen as surplus to the system of social reproduction. So homosexuality is literally seen as a negation of life force and creativity. In his essay "Tearooms and Sympathy," Lee Edelman quotes from a homophobic essay by Norman Mailer as part of a subsection entitled "On Waste": " 'If excrement is the enforced marriage of Tragic Beauty and Filth, why then did God desert it, and leave our hole to the Devil, unless it is because God has hegemony over us as we create each other. God owns the creation, but the Devil has power over all we waste—how natural for him to lay siege where the body ends and weak tragic air begins' " (1992, 278).

Commenting on the blatant homophobia of Mailer's statement, Edelman notes how in Mailer's essay "heterosexuality alone possesses the divine attribute of creativity here; homosexual activity, by contrast, leads only to waste, as Mailer insisted in an interview in 1962: 'I think one of the reasons that homosexuals go through such agony when they're around 40 or 50 is that their lives have nothing to do with procreation. . . . They've used up their being' " (Edelman 1992, 278). Likewise, in her essay on the sexualized nature of urban consumption, Gillian Swanson notes how waste metaphors are important in articulating the distinction between sex and commerce: "the correspondence of sex and commercial city life was produced through a concept of waste, then, whose inscription on the bodies of men was a story about the new relations of commerce in city life" (1995, 85). She quotes from David Walker's work on the relationship between discourses of waste in Australian national identity: "If masturbation represented the unproductive expenditure of energy in the individual, likewise the city was commonly regarded as wasteful of human energies. . . . 'The cities . . . exhausted and diminished their inhabitants. Exhaustion became the symbol of what was assumed to be a troubling imbalance between the high expenditure of energy and a low personal reward' " (85). Same-sex activity is thus seen as wasteful, as surplus to production. Moreover, in the current climate, it becomes equated with death. The homophobic equating of male homosexuality with death has intensified since the onset of AIDS. The unsafe exchange of bodily fluids is most clearly tainted with the mark of death. Since AIDS, death and desire are impossible to separate. In order to have safer sex, we must be aware of our own mortality.

The Museum's Ruins

Ruins are a common motif in current writing about the urban. There is a wide reflection of an urban impasse: in the urban landscape, we see the destruction wrought by postindustrialism, by post-Fordism—decaying factories, derelict wasteland, and empty spaces. For example, Patrick Wright's book on 1980s London is entitled *Journey Through Ruins* (1991). Ruins feature prominently in the work of cultural critic Douglas Crimp. It is intriguing that Crimp has also written about the devastating effect of AIDS in representation, art, and culture. One wonders what the links are between death and urban space in light of this connection. Crimp's famous essay "On the Museum's Ruins" is concerned with death and space

(Crimp 1993a)—specifically the means by which museums have died as spaces where cultural production was concentrated and monopolized. Postmodernism has exploded the distinctions between high and low culture, so the institutions that were once arbiters of cultural taste and the buildings that housed their choices have become defunct: a death has occurred in museum culture. I wonder what role gay men have had in taking culture out of museums (where our art has been and still is excluded on the basis of its capacity to shock and disgust) and onto the streets, into urban space (see, for example, work on the use of art and graphics in AIDS activism; Crimp and Rolston 1990).

Crimp discusses the conflict over photographer Robert Mapplethorpe in the United States, where his SM photographs became the center of one of the most heated debates in U.S. cultural politics. The far right, led by Jesse Helms, attempted to sabotage a National Endowment for the Arts funding bill to prevent public money being spent on "pornography." The point that Crimp makes is that "The line that Mapplethorpe crossed, between the safely homosocial and the dangerously homosexual, was also a line between the aesthetics of traditional museum culture and the prerogatives of a self-defining gay subculture" (1993b, 7). The bounded space of the museum was a container for exotic otherness, which like other institutions of modern life, excluded any form of sexual dissident subjectivity. The space of the museum has been and still is hostile toward overt displays of sexuality.

Crimp argues that traditional museum culture has excluded overt homosexuality; it has not been open to the demands of its gay citizens. It is specifically gay eroticism that must be circumscribed and excluded completely from within the walls of the museum. This censorship is ultimately impossible given that sexual dissident viewers and audiences can locate queer meanings within homosocial traditions. Thus, the museum's containment of queerness is futile because even the most homosocial spaces are vulnerable to queer reading (football terraces, rugby pitches, the military). Crimp notes how in the defense of Mapplethorpe's art the museum sought to assimilate and annihilate the eroticism of the work by deploying formalist arguments about the work's technical merit (thereby denying its troubling queerness). The Mapplethorpe case, then, throws important light onto the question of eroticism and representation in the traditional space of high culture—the museum.

In his essay "Aversion/Perversion/Diversion," Samuel Delany argues

that we have not yet begun to articulate the sexual landscape in language—
which we must do in order to be more precise in our work on sexuality:

> the bulk of the extraordinarily rich, fragmenting, and complex sexual
> landscape has been—and remains—outside of language. Most of it will
> remain there quite some time. . . . But what is not articulated in certain or-
> ders of language—written language, say, and of a certain formality—does
> not mean that it doesn't exist. Nor does it mean that its effects as a perva-
> sive context do not inform other articulations that either do not reflect it
> directly—or that reflect only a highly coded, heavily policed fraction of it.
> . . . What is accepted into language at any level is *always* different at differ-
> ent places and in different periods. . . . The sexual experience is *still*
> largely outside language at least as it (language) is constituted at any
> number of levels. (1995, 28–32, emphasis in original)

Delany's own work has explored the boundaries of eroticism and representation. It is therefore unsurprising that his work has been vulnerable
to the accusation that it reifies experience. It is significant that his utopian
description of his experience of public sexual democracy and sexual awak-
ening in a men's bathroom has been attacked for essentialism. In her essay
"The Evidence of Experience," for example, Joan Scott (1993) argues that
Delany's work is problematic in this regard. Nevertheless, his insightful
comments on the limits of representation are valuable in the context of exploring the relationship between the material and the imaginary in the
context of "urban desires."

Real Space and Fantasy Space

Sexual dissidents are acutely aware of space in our everyday lives because
we constantly have to re-create it from nothing. Heterosexual space and
heterosexual desire are all-pervasive—just *there*. Heterosexual identity is
ubiquitous and thereby *placeless*. In this sense, queer space is intimately dependent on a sense *for* place for its realization. For example, David Woodhead (1995) reminds us that cottages (tearooms) are ephemeral places
subject to change by word of mouth, reputation, and above all *gossip*. Not
every public toilet is a cottage, in the same way that not every canalside
towpath or urban wasteground is a cruising zone. These pleasure grounds
are fragile, ephemeral, *soft*. The softness of the city is reflected in the plas-

ticity of queer imagination and longing, as Michael Bronski notes: "The relationship between sexual fantasy and sexual reality is never simple. . . . The gay imagination seems to be never-ending, always capable of invention and qualification in its search for pleasure, responding to our emotional needs as well as to our sexual and physical experiences" (1991, 64).

Perhaps there is an element of utopianism in Bronski's celebration of the never-ending creative potential of the gay imagination (see also Bell, chapter 4 in this volume). Surely not all gay men are free to develop such a rich vocabulary of pleasure: What about race, class, and disability? In his essay, intriguingly subtitled "Notes on the Materialization of Sexual Fantasy," Bronski earlier argues that *Fantasies allow us to create a context and a space for our desires.* When we act out these fantasies, we, in a sense, kill them off. They are no longer 'safe' because they have materialized into the world in which belts and whips hurt, emotions are complicated, and other people have to be paid attention to" (1991, 62, my emphasis).

The distinction between reality and fantasy corresponds to a distinction between real space and fantasy space. Queer space is ephemeral, constructed by desire in the first place. I had desires about places and people before I ever had a chance to realize them. I always dreamed of the city as the space where these desires would be materialized. In the same way, Paul Hallam reflects on his childhood in Mansfield: "Sodom was an idea, a place, long before I connected it with specific acts" (1993, 70). Sexualized places are where desires are materialized. But desire in turn impacts on the physical, material urban environment. Without desire and fantasy, there would be no apartment blocks, no gay gentrification, no gay bars and cafés, and no gay villages. As Bronski writes, fantasies can be empowering: "Without the possibility of becoming reality, a fantasy is of no use whatsoever. Fantasy draws its potential from the fact that it can, might become real. It is precisely at this moment the crossover when fantasy become reality—that we experience the power we can have over our own lives" (1991, 63).

Since the onset of AIDS, certain material realities have been put off-limits—the material reality of fucking another man without a condom, sex without fear. It is unsurprising in light of this change that many younger gay men express nostalgia for a lost Golden Age before the threat of AIDS. With the onset of AIDS and safer sex, fantasies have become more central in our discussions of sex and erotic play. Place has become central to our fantasy in a culture laden with loss and melancholia. Perhaps the most haunting passage in Paul Hallam's Sodom Circuit Walk is when he reflects on the impact of death on the surfeit of secondhand books on Sodom:

> Some days I'll wander from the stalls to bookshops, looking for second-hand Sodoms, for more obvious and directly related books, for Sodom studies. . . . One of the slightly chill experiences of late is the sometimes obvious explanation behind the bulging "new in stock" shelves. New stock after deaths. My local second-hand bookseller confirmed what I'd already suspected: the sixties porn that he'd like to clear had belonged to a man who had recently died. . . . Once cherished pin-ups now dumped in the corner, unadmired. Gay's the Word bookshop [in London] recently replenished its stock after a funeral. (1993, 36)

The sadness in this passage reflects a profound sense of loss—of bodies missing from the city, remembered only through their now-discarded books. This sense of loss brought about by AIDS has profoundly affected queer culture in countless ways, from scenes of public mourning to the embodied rage of activists. But AIDS has also reoriented the politics of pleasure.

Fantasies, Spaces, Bodies

Bronski lists ten notes on the materialization of desire. Point number ten is: *"The explosion of private sexual fantasy into public view is a powerful political statement.* In a world that functions on sexual repression, the sight of two queens or dykes walking down the street is a vision of the gradual cracking of the social order. *The drag queen, the butch lesbian, the clone, the lipstick lesbian, are all expositions of sexual dreams—waking nightmares for the culture at large"* (1991, 64, my emphasis). Here Bronski argues that these bodies contest the public/private divide; they contest the social order. Here leather drag is oppositional—a form of resistance to the heterosexual ordering of things. Bronski does admit to some ambivalence in that drag's subversiveness may not be understood as such (by the straight world); nevertheless, for Bronski, leather drag is empowering. He argues that it challenges the definition of space as straight: "The blatant, public image of the leather man (or woman) is an outright threat to the existing, although increasingly dysfunctional, system of gender arrangements and sexual repression under which we have all lived. 'This is our power,' we are saying, 'and the power is ours to do with what we please. It was always ours and we have reclaimed it for our own use and our own pleasure" (1991, 64).

Bronski reflects on his own sexual self-image and how he has become the man of his dreams, asking, "How did this image of myself get out from inside my head (where I suspect it had been for a very long time) and into the actual, material world? . . . At any given moment our fantasy image might change depending on what we need. This is especially true of sexual self-images" (57).

Concerning the visibility of leather/SM cultures, Geoff Mains notes in his book *Urban Aboriginals* that "in the Gay/Lesbian sub-cultures, garments and even toys become symbols carried well beyond the area of play to the open light of public spaces," adding that such "props" "speak of a tribal affiliation that is as strongly social as it is sexual" (1984, 175; see also Holliday, chapter 3 in this volume). For Mains, leathersex is assertive, strong, and social rather than a pitiful reflection of the internalized hatred and shame of an isolated individual going to an invisible backstreet leather bar. Mains celebrates leatherspace as social and public rather than private and domesticated (on the suburban, domesticated image of SM, see Bell in this volume).

Leatherspaces are highly specialized and localized geographically. The South of Market (SOMA) area of San Francisco became the greatest concentration of leather bars in the United States. This area is the most documented, and its community the most sophisticated but also the most heavily affected by AIDS. The sexual geography of SOMA has changed out of all recognition in light of the impacts of AIDS and of economic restructuring in the city, which is further marginalizing already pushed-out sexual spaces (Rubin 1998).

Sadomasochism and Urban Desire

Loyalty to and hunger for place are among the keenest of city feelings,
reverenced and prized precisely because they go against the grain of that drift
towards the formless and unstable which the city seems to encourage in us.
—Jonathan Raban, *Soft City*

Sadomasochism is very much a marker of urban life. The *public* stages of SM are to be found in very few localities within large cities. John Lee notes the prevalence of gay male SM territories in metropolitan North America:

"The gay communities of most large North American cities now facilitate the first encounters of men seeking partners for S&M sex through three specialized territories: the leather bar, the leather baths and the leather club. . . . One significant observation is that the leather bar is even more a defended home territory than the ordinary gay bar. Those who enter without the accepted dress and demeanor are likely to be made to feel unwelcome" (1983, 180–81).

Lee's essay was written before the dawning of the full awful reality of the AIDS pandemic. Since the onset of AIDS, the leather/SM scene has had to fight for its survival. As one of the most overtly sexual of lifestyles, sadomasochism has been most prone to vilification and attack. Pat Califia stresses that SM territories can never be taken for granted. They don't just exist; they have to be defended against the forces of moral conservatism:

> Leather bars, clubs, and dungeons are the places where fetishists and sadomasochists meet, relax, find new friends and lovers, play, and create a community. Many of these places are far from perfect. They are often fire hazards—Mafia-run, dirty, small and overpriced. But without them we would be even more marginalized, even more isolated. We can never take this space for granted. We have to simultaneously defend, occupy, expand, guide others to, and hide our territory if we are going to a survive as a people. (1994, 17)

What is notable about Califia's argument is the clear awareness of the importance of space to the construction of SM scenes, communities, and identities, and of the need to strive to survive.

In some writing on the city, there is a tendency to represent SM as the Other—as a marker of the exotic extremes of urban living. Consider this extraordinary example taken from Richard Sennett's *The Conscience of the Eye* (1991). Sennett narrates a walk around his neighborhood in Manhattan, which is evidently populated with all manner of urban exotica, including leather bars. What is noticeable here is Sennett's maintenance of distance from the scenes he experiences, as witnessed by his use of "they" and "them" and his depiction of "men with careful eyes." This distancing gives us the clues we need:

> The middle-Twenties [in Manhattan] play host as well to a group of bars that cater to these leather fetishists, bars in run-down townhouses with no

signs and blacked-out windows. What makes the middle-Twenties distinct is that all the customers in the leather shops are served alike—rudely.
Saddles and whips are sold by harassed salesmen, wrapped by clerks os-
tentatiously bored. Nor do the horsey matrons seem to care much where
the men with careful eyes take their purchases, no curiosity about the
blacked-out windows from behind which ooze the smells of beer, leather,
and urine. A city of differences, and of fragments of life that do not connect: in such a city the obsessed are set free. (1991, 125)

Sennett concludes the description with a phobic statement calculated to exclude, to Other. For him, sadomasochism and leather bars are symptoms of
urban living, proof that city life "liberates" deviance. He states that urban
life is characterized by "fragments . . . that do not connect." It would be
more accurate to argue that city life simply facilitates the mixing and match-
ing of lifestyles. Who is to say that these fragments do not connect? From
my own perspective, there is nothing special or fragmented about a daily
round of supermarket, leather bar, library, deli, bookshop—because they
are the places where I feel more or less comfortable. The notion that SMers
are "obsessed" represents a pathologizing of SM sexuality. Against this
(phobic) argument that SM represents urban life beyond the limit, Edmund
White boldly proclaims the urban Amercian SM culture of the pre-AIDS
1980s as pioneering: "If it didn't sound too much like gay chauvinism, I'd
suggest that gays have often pioneered the frontiers of urban single life.
Gay fashions quickly become Fashion, and gay sado-masochism may por-
tend yet another trend among straights" (1995 [1979], 57).

In her essay "The City of Desire: Its Anatomy and Destiny," Pat Califia
writes eloquently about the so-called sex zones of the city. By this term, she
means the spaces within the city where sex is bought and sold, and where
marginal sexual minorities make their home. She makes a number of interesting points about sexuality and urban space; reflecting Gayle Rubin's hierarchy of "acceptable" sexual desires, Califia argues that

> The city is a map of the hierarchy of desire, from the valorized to the stig-
> matised. It is divided into zones dictated by the way its citizens value or
> denigrate their needs. Separating the city into areas of specialisation
> makes it possible to meet some needs more efficiently; it is also an attempt
> to reduce conflict between opposing sets of desires and the roles people
> adapt to try to fulfill those desires. . . . The sex zone does not have an in-
> dependent existence; no area of the city is dedicated solely to this use. It is

usually superimposed upon another area: a deteriorating neighborhood where poor people, especially those who have recently arrived in the city, must live; an area that has very few residents because it is designed to manufacture or transport goods; or one of those offerings to eco-guilt, a city park. (1994, 205)

The sex zone lies in marginal space—the zone of transition. We cannot understand the changing political-economic fortunes of these areas without simultaneously understanding transformations in the gay scene. Thus, the 1990s Gay Village in Manchester, England, has been transformed from being sleazy to being respectable thanks to incoming capital investment (see Bell in this volume). Folsom Street in San Francisco has also been transformed from being a depopulated warehousing district to being the heart of the San Francisco avant-garde. Although leather cultures have been highly influential in the recoding of these spaces as desirable, those cultures are crowded out as property values escalate (Rubin 1998). Overt displays of queer SM sexuality are replaced by cappuccino culture. In this regard, Califia has some fascinating things to say about *invisibility* and *surplus value:*

Despite the fact that people are willing to pay inflated prices for sex zone products, even its most compulsive customers pretend that everything for sale there is trivial, worthless and unnecessary. They pretend, in fact, that this marketplace does not exist at all. So a sex zone must acquire at least a token invisibility to avoid threatening its customers as well as the authorities. This means that if one visits a sex zone at the wrong time of day, it may be unrecognizable. This type of market-place is usually tolerated only between sunset and dawn. (1994, 206)

The nighttime economy has largely been overlooked in the study of sexuality and space (with the exception of work on prostitution, perhaps). The use of queer space at the margins of the day creates particular problems in terms of safety, of course. Further, the different uses of space at different times of the day stress the ephemeral nature of these spaces, which really come into their own only at night (although the blossoming of daytime continental café culture has meant that gay time has been extended with all-day openings).

Set against this glamorizing of queer consumption practices in Gay

Villages, sadomasochism trades in the least commodifiable of signs. Part of the SM lifestyle is *eroticization of dirt, decay, dereliction*. Again, this specific eroticization could be interpreted as part of internalized gay self-hatred, but I think it is simply more pragmatic. Thus, a leather bar that is decidedly down-at-heel and in an unsafe area may prove more of a turn-on. Part of the *jouissance* of going to such a space may be the thrill of occupying a space one is not meant to be in—the thrill of danger and excitement of parking one's car in a dangerous part of town.

Of course, for the scene queens with less money, the real danger is in territorializing leather desire. How you get to the bar says a lot about what kind of queen you are. Using public transport implies dangers—putting yourself at greater risk than patrons who roll up to the front door of a club in expensive cars or taxis. Wearing leather or fetish gear on public transport means risking homophobia—especially on weekend evenings when straight lads are out to show how hard they are by queerbashing.

SM and the City

What is the link between SM culture and the city, then? What is it about urban life that fosters the growth of SM culture? Jonathan Raban's *Soft City* may provide us with some ideas. Comparing Jonathan Raban's with David Harvey's imagining of the city, Paul Patton argues that "The important difference from Harvey's account is that Raban refuses to draw a distinction between the imaginary city and its real conditions of existence. The city itself is 'soft,' in the sense that it is a type of reality for which the boundary between imagination and fact is not absolute" (1995, 116).

Central to Raban's imagination is the concept of the city as melodrama. I have noted that SM culture elevates the theatrical and the performative, and the city is therefore the natural backdrop for sexual experimentation. The plasticity of the city discussed by Raban enables the development of "marginal" cultures:

> Cities, unlike villages and small towns, are plastic by nature. We mould them in our images: they, in their turn, shape us by the resistance they offer when we try to impose our own personal form on them. . . . The city as we imagine it, the soft city of illusion, myth, aspiration, nightmare, is as real, maybe more real, than the hard city one can locate on maps, in statis-

tics, in monographs on urban sociology and demography and architecture. . . . If a city can estrange you from yourself, how much more powerfully can it detach you from the lives of other people, and how deeply immersed you may become in the inaccessibly private community of your own head. (Raban 1974, 2)

In *The Book of Sodom*, Paul Hallam provides us with a guide to his own city, noting that "My walk is in London, but I drift across time, across place. It could be a walk in almost any city. Any city worth its salt has been called at one time or other, Sodom" (1993, 15). Hallam bemoans the clean-cut image of Queer Soho, wondering whether the roughness of desire has been ironed-out here:

I might explain why I find the mushrooming of smart gay cafe bars in Soho so alarming, a gay village (small town, Zoar) that looks less and less like Sodom, more and more like the cleaned-up Covent Garden. A sanitised Sodom. Sodom clean and cold, with fake class. Out, the decay, the smutty and the sleaze . . . I want neither bricks nor brimstone. No return to the fears of the fifties, the closed-curtain clubs. It's just that I miss Satyricon Sodom. Sodom circuit-walks should take in alleyways, dark passages, stone steps down. I'm wary of the clean and pure, and all that is done in their name. Leave a few corners dark, not designer dark, but plain. (1993, 44–45)

From Hallam's call to leave a few corners dark, I want now to move on to explore representations of London's dark corners, first off with a look at the work of pulp-splatter fiction writer Stewart Home.

The Urban Pornotopia of Stewart Home's London: "Sexual Violence and Violent Sex"

I need to preface my discussion of Stewart Home's writing on the body in the city by considering the writer whose work served as Home's inspiration—Richard Allen. Richard Allen was one of the pen names of James Moffat, a Canadian writer of pulp fiction who was employed by the publishers New English Library to write books on youth subcultures targeted at the youth market. In the late 1960s and early 1970s, Allen wrote a number of works of pulp fiction on the theme of skinheads. The most popular and most influential was *Skinhead,* published in 1970, which detailed the exploits of Joe Hawkins, an East End skinhead. *Skinhead* sold more than one hundred thousand copies in the early 1970s and was reprinted numerous times, most recently in the early 1990s. Other novels in a similar mold followed, including *Suedehead, Skinhead Girls,* and *Boot Boys.*

Joe Hawkins was Allen's main protagonist. As the archetypal thug, he took great pleasure in getting involved in rucks—beating up anyone who got in his way. His major pleasures involved racist and homophobic violence and rough (hetero)sex. Hawkins took great pride in his skinhead identity and the hardness of his appearance:

> Opening the wardrobe, he selected his gear from its shadowy recesses. . . . Union shirt—collarless and identical to thousands of others worn by his kind throughout the country; army trousers and braces; and boots! The boots were the most important item. Without his boots, he was part of the common-herd. . . . Joe was proud of *his* boots. His were genuine army-disposal boots; thick-soled, studded, heavy to wear and heavy to feel if slammed against a rib. (Allen 1992, 14, emphasis in original)

As an East Ender, Joe takes great pleasure in his Cockney identity, proclaiming Cockney pride despite his contempt for the squalor of his native Plaistow. Hawkins feels that the "Cockney nation" is under threat from forces from elsewhere. The racist Joe Hawkins bemoans the decline of Cockney power:

> The Cockney had lost control of his London. Even Soho had gone down the drain of provincial invasion. The pimps and touts weren't old-established Londoner types. They came from Scouseland, Malta, Cyprus and Jamaica. Even the porno shops were having their difficulties with the parasitic influx of outside talent. . . . The old cockney thug was slowly being confined—to Bow, Mile End, Bethnal Green and their fringe areas. London was wide open now. To anyone with a gun, a cosh, an army of thugs. (15)

Allen had a highly ambivalent position toward skinheads, arguing for greater control and punishment of unruly or subversive groups in society, his opinions reflecting the moral panic surrounding skinheads in the 1970s—which he also cashed into with his books. Skinheads functioned as the "enemy within" in the early 1970s in the attempt to bolster up postcolonial English identity at a time of profound social, economic, and political crisis. Allen clearly saw his work as contributing toward a more authoritarian view of law and order; by exposing the supposed excesses of skinhead subculture, he sought to publicize their behavior so that the authorities would do something to crack down on this particular unruly youth cult, arguing that the English state must deploy violence to punish anarchic youth. As a highly visible youth cult, the skinheads made an easy scapegoat for the authorities. In this context, it is highly ironic that skinheads adopted Joe Hawkins as one of their own and that the Richard Allen books became a part of skinhead folklore. In *Spirit of '69: A Skinhead Bible*, George Marshall notes that Joe Hawkins was "probably the most famous skinhead of them all" (1991, 54). Marshall, a self-proclaimed authority on the skinhead cult, republished a number of Richard Allen's skinhead stories as omnibuses. Although doubtful of the authenticity of Allen's account of skinhead culture, Marshall celebrates Hawkins's sexual exploits and violence: "Reading about Joe having sex every other chapter, and him beating someone up in between, was the stuff skinhead dreams were made of . . . and give Richard Allen his due. He couldn't have been that clueless to document the changing phases of skinhead, even if his books were a little short on detail in the style and music departments. Still, what did it matter who was on the radio, just as long as you got a dose of soft-porn when Joe mounted his latest conquest?" (1991, 54).

As well as being overtly racist and sexist, Allen's main protagonists are blatantly straight and celebrated sexual conquests alongside success in fights. There is absolutely no hint of sexual ambiguity in Joe Hawkins. In *Skinhead*, he is the personification of hardness: "Basically Joe Hawkins had a 'feeling' for violence. Regardless of what the do-gooders and the socialists and psychiatrists claimed some people had an instinct bent on creating havoc and resorting to jungle savagery. Joe was one of these" (Allen 1992, 160). Allen's legacy lives on, reappropriated and recycled by a new crowd of pulp-fiction writers, the most notable of whom is Stewart Home (see also Bell and Binnie 1998).

Stewart Home's Experimental Writing

Stewart Home is an experimental novelist who has written a number of novels on themes of urban anarchy, disaffection, and violent sexuality. His first novel, *Pure Mania,* was published in 1989. This work was followed by *Defiant Pose* in 1991, a collection of short stories—*No Pity*—in 1993, and more novels, *Red London* in 1994 and *Slow Death* in 1996. In addition to his novels, Home has written widely on Situationist thought and has championed the experimental and subversive in contemporary political philosophy. For example, instead of the usual assertion of the author's moral right to be identified as the author of the work, in *No Pity* Home playfully "asserts his moral right to be identified as a rampant plagiarist bent on reinventing world culture in its entirety" (1993, 2). Home's blending of anarchism and Situationism is an important context to bear in mind when approaching his work. Home has written widely on plagiarism and has experimented with different ways of writing, and his writing style is self-referential. If we accept that camp defuses the distinctions between high and low culture and undermines established cultural authorities and arbiters of taste, then Stewart Home's writing can definitely be considered camp. He mixes the high seriousness of cultural theory with trashy porn to produce a camp perspective on city life. As Iain Sinclair says on the dust jacket of *Slow Death* (1996): "It is an exercise in futility to complain that Home's novels lack depth, characterization or complex plots: that is the whole point. The project operates within its contradictions, subverting the spirit of redundant industrial fiction, while honouring the form. . . . Home's language feeds on metropolitan restlessness, movement, lists of trains and buses, gigs in pubs, rucks outside phone kiosks, the epiphany of the greasey caff."

Home takes delight in setting different writing styles off against one another, juxtaposing high cultural theory with pornographic writing on the pleasures of the body to produce a frisson of recognition and pleasure. In particular, the juxtaposition of disembodied Marxist economic theories on surplus value and exchange with porn featuring the exchange of bodily fluids produces a sense of *jouissance,* as this passage from the short story "Anarchist" demonstrates: "Butcher entered the kitchen, unseen as Dog and Steve vainly attempted to erase the marks of value and exchange inscribed on their bodies by capital and its glistening commodities, as unaware as Butcher that the 'naturalness' of their sexual practice was as carefully constructed by the agents of recuperation as the anarchist ideology they embraced" (Home 1993, 43). In *Pure Mania,* as the anarchist pub band Alienation mouths the words to their song "Destroy the Family," Home comments: "The chords of the chorus were not dissimilar to the opening bars of the Sex Pistols' Anarchy in the UK. The words were pieced together from Angry Brigade communiques, Situationist texts and Deleuze and Guattari's Anti-Oedipus" (1989, 195).

This passage could be a corrective to the high seriousness of intellectual debates about Deleuze and Guattari's ideas. One does not normally encounter Deleuze and Guattari in the lyrics of punk records! Home acknowledges a debt to Situationist thought, which sought to bring about "The Revolution of Everyday Life" by bringing attention to the psychogeographical experience of urban space—to demonstrate how the forces of capital condition and commodify everyday life. Writers such as Guy Debord critiqued the utopian rationality of 1960s urban geography and planning for ignoring the place of desire in the urban experience (see Bell, this volume). Central to the psychogeography that Situationists promoted was the notion of the *dérive* or drift. The *dérive* enabled desire to be linked to buildings and specific aspects of the urban landscape. As Sadie Plant writes, "To *dérive* was to notice the way in which certain areas, streets, or buildings resonate with states of mind, inclinations, and desires, and to seek out reasons for movement other than those for which an environment was designed. It was very much a matter of using an environment for one's own ends, seeking not only the marvellous beloved by surrealism, but bringing an inverted perspective to bear on the entirety of the spectacular world" (1992, 59).

To promote spontaneous urban pleasure and challenge the spectacle, Home blends Situationist praxis with the resonances attached to the experience of the East End in Richard Allen's novels. He clearly models himself on Richard Allen. Like Allen, Home boasts of churning out his novels in a few days. One clue to Stewart Home's perspective on Richard Allen can be found in Home's novel *Pure Mania*, in which one of his characters, Chickenfeed, makes reference to Richard Allen's style of pulp fiction:

> His writing had been of the generic, and unsaleable, boy-in-the-bedroom variety until he'd had one of those flashes of inspiration common to men of genius. He'd decided to produce an updated survey of the territory Richard Allen explored in the early and mid-seventies. . . . Chickenfeed wrote to a strict formula. He read and reread Allen's novels taking note of key phrases and narrative techniques. Then he set to work on his own book, incorporating the Allen style but updating it, referring to fashionable brand names and the latest trends. (Home 1989, 22)

However, whereas Richard Allen's Joe Hawkins clearly lacks a politicized class consciousness, Home's anarchist protagonist Terry Blake is a working-class hero and hedonist: "Terry was a boot-boy, a skinhead, a working-class warrior who was ready and able to take on all those who would oppress him with their determinist doctrines" (Home 1991, 47). Moreover, Terry challenges the moralism of liberal political correctness: "As a skinhead, Terry was justly proud of his severe appearance. To the bourgeoisie, his cropped hair made him featureless and thus less than an individual. In a sense, this rendered him anonymous and invisible. . . . Terry's appearance aroused moral indignation, which led innumerable trendies to fantasize about possessing him. They wanted to fuck, and be fucked by someone who rejected plastic individualism" (49). It is specifically Home's *detournement* of Richard Allen, Home's writing on the eroticization of body and city, and the deployment of violence in his eroticization of the city on which I wish to focus my discussion now.

Home's *Detournement* of Allen's Sex and Violence

In Situationist thinking, the desire for spontaneous acts of subversion to challenge the commodification of everyday experience led to the tactic of *detournement*—a tactic for creating new subjective experiences of space outside of market relations. Sadie Plant defines *detournement* as "a turning around and a reclamation of lost meaning: a way of putting the stasis of the spectacle in motion. It is plagiaristic, because its materials are those which already appear within the spectacle, and subversive, since its tactics are those of the 'reversal of perspective,' a challenge to meaning aimed at the context in which it arises" (1992, 86).

We see evidence of the *detournement* of Richard Allen's work in Home's writing, particularly in the context of sexuality and violence. The major protagonists in Allen's books are straight, but in Home's they are polymorphously perverse. Home's protagonists embrace consensual SM and reject the censorial political views of anarchist and left groups. They also reject pro-censorship, anti-SM feminist writers; for example, in *Defiant Pose,* the bootboy Terry Blake describes a sex scene with Gloria Patterson: "Gloria had taken him home and he'd actually consented to tying her up before they had sex. Unlike her comrades in the anarchist movement, the skinhead had never once suggested that her S & M deviationism was a degrading submission to the norms of patriarchal society" (Home 1991, 143).

Home's *detournement* of Allen also extends to writing the urban. For Richard Allen, it was the city that bred hooligans and violent characters such as Joe Hawkins: "Joe had a feeling for violence. It was an integral part of his make-up. Some do-gooders trying to explain his attachment to the skinhead cult would no doubt, stress his environmental background, his childhood fighting for every scrap of education and clothing. They would point with undisguised delight to his father's tough profession, to the East End as a breeding-ground of crime and the conditions under which its inhabitants grew up" (Allen 1992, 41).

This view of the city as a breeding ground for violent unlawful masculinity—still prominent in popular discourses of the "underclass" and working class—is turned on its head in Stewart Home's novels, which embody a Situationist perspective on the urban as the site of spontaneous pleasure. In Situationist thought, the city is to be reclaimed from the rationality of planning and from the programmed pleasures of consumer capitalism by spontaneous acts of hedonism to forge subversive practices of everyday life. Allen's writing on the city reflects the view of the early 1970s that rational planning must eradicate the dirt and decay of the slums. Home overturns the authoritarianism of Allen's nightmare view of the city, where bodies are out of control, by aestheticizing decay, waste, and dereliction. In *Skinhead*, Joe Hawkins detests the East End and wants a "posh flat" in Mayfair. On a train leaving Victoria Station for Brighton, he reflects on his London:

> Slowly at first, then gathering speed, the train moved out of the station, the crumbling warehouses and dilapidated homes along the track like sicknesses on the face of London. Joe didn't see the horror of railway surroundings. Nothing here was worse than his own neighbourhood; nothing worse than Plaistow or Poplar. Although he had ambitions to rise above the filth of working-class districts, he had accepted conditions with the fatalism of those born to squalor. It was one thing to believe in a West End flat, a Mayfair bird, a gleaming car and new gear every day of the week, but the brainwashed mind could not see further than personal betterment. It couldn't realise that all of this slumland must be cleared and kept free from decay. It couldn't accept that people had to be educated to

have pride in their surroundings, to make their district forever clean and fresh and on a par with other high-class areas. (Allen 1992, 40)

Further, Hawkins detests tradition, taking joy in the modern, ugly buildings of the city; as Allen writes, "None of the monuments nor architectural beauties made any impression on Joe. He was ignorant of historical heritage, believing in modern sterile skyscrapers as the ultimate in construction" (27). Home's characters take pleasure in a similar antiaesthetic structure of feeling. The grimy postindustrial landscape of East London and the modern ugly buildings of the city form the backdrop for their violent escapades—beating up racists and fascists, and enjoying violent sex. Home's characters have sex in the ruins of London, but are always conscious of living under capitalist social relations.

The Queer Context of Home's Writing

Home's heroes are, as already stated, polymorphously perverse. Whereas Joe Hawkins's politics are authoritarian and blatantly racist, sexist, and homophobic, Home's heroes are libertarian anarchists. In an interview in U.K. "style magazine" *i-D*, Home comments on his story "New Britain," arguing that "The story is playing the skinhead theme against the gay theme. . . . Gay skinheads are great because they totally upset people's notions of what a skinhead should be. We also challenge the ridiculous idea that skinhead equals racism, which it clearly doesn't. The skinhead came out of the whole mod thing, which came out of Afro-Caribbean culture" (Cornwell 1993, 107). In his book *Gay Skins*, Murray Healy acknowledges the queerying of Richard Allen in Stewart Home's novels. He argues that gay skinheads' use of Allen's texts to feed their sexual fantasies would have mortified the morally conservative Allen: "The anarchist London of Home's novels, the queer activities of his skin heroes, and a culture where such appropriations are not so much feasible as inevitable, hardly constitute the kind of tradition Allen would have wanted the conservative political vision of his books to inspire" (1996, 100).

Whereas Allen's stories are notorious for their racism and homophobia, Home's are antiracist and queer. Allen's Joe Hawkins beats up a queer in Soho; Home has queers fucking like rabbits in highly stylized, theatrical urban settings. The sex in Home's novels is hysterical, ultracamp: his protagonists wave their "fuck sticks," which shoot "genetic wads of liquid

DNA." The most shocking aspect of the way sex is represented in Home's novels is not the violence or polymorphous perversity, but rather the prevalence of bodily fluids and their unsafe exchange. Home wrote his novels after the emergence of AIDS, so it is shocking that the sex (and there is a lot of it in his novels) is so unsafe. But I would suggest that Home's novels should be read as a pornographic supplement, as safer sex, as one-handed reading. They help provide queer erotic pleasures in the city at a time when these pleasures are being restricted by law.

Home's writing on the city and its polymorphous pleasures has, surprisingly, received little attention outside of its specialist readership. One writer to make extensive use of Home's work, however, is Iain Sinclair, who enjoys a much higher profile than Home as a documentor of London's underside. His books *Downriver* (1991) and *Lights Out for the Territory* (1997) chart a similarly paranoid cartography of contemporary London. *Downriver* received widespread critical acclaim within literary circles for its depiction of the maelstrom of violent flows and energies of contemporary London life, encapsulated in the title, with one reviewer describing it as a "Brilliant poetic dissection of the squalor, greed, criminality and madness of both super- and sub-structure of London today" (dust jacket). Like Home, Sinclair produces work that explores the materiality of urban space free from the constraints of academic discipline. Both writers share a concern with the conceit of truth, playing with the distinction between truth and fiction, fantasy and reality.

In *Lights Out for the Territory*, Sinclair refines his exploration of the materiality of past and present Londons. In this book, subtitled *9 Excursions in the Secret History of London*, there is more of an attempt to create or impose some order on the chaos articulated in *Downriver*. The book is structured around these nine journeys, which Sinclair shares with fellow explorers of the materiality of London. He meets other writers who have sought to name and describe the experiences of (dis)location, desire, and identity within contemporary London. Stewart Home is one of these writers. Sinclair discusses Home's ideas throughout *Lights Out*, but specifically when he is narrating his experiences of Dalston, Stoke Newington, and Mile End. He states his admiration for Home's projects:

> by 1995 he was essentially the *only* (unelected) representative of the avant-garde left. . . . He was the Beaverbrook of the counter-culture: *Smile, The London Psychogeographical Association Newsletter, Neoist Alliance* flyers,

multiple identity black propaganda, squibs planted in the press, samizdat leaflets shot through significant letterboxes by the bicycling author. The man existed in a rush of paranoid, Masonic conspiracy excavations: the problem was finding new locations in which to have himself photographed. Home sustained a programme that would have exhausted a less committed self-publicist: readings, lectures, club performances, essays, postal art, videos, expositions of historical avant-garde tendencies, creative plagiarism, denunciations, feuds, schisms, occult investigations, post-pulp novels, demolitions of those innocent mainstreamers who were getting more attention than he was. (1997, 221)

Sinclair praises Home's depictions of Hackney not for their historical accuracy or truthfulness, but for their very contrived nature. He also praises Home's duplicity, calling him "a marvellously untrustworthy (by intent) historian of this Interzone" (1997, 29).

By depicting events the way Home does, he is able to locate a truth not found within urban history or the heritage industry. Sinclair argues that Home's extravagant fictions are in fact closer approximations to the truth of the place than other "serious" accounts. "His fictions become the most reasonable approximations to the truth. Misheard asides mature to full-blown rumours. Pub whispers infiltrate gossip columns, feed back on the Secret State controllers" (1997, 221).

I explore this question of truth in depth elsewhere (Binnie 1997a). I examine the contention that camp is a queer subversion of the notion of the universality of truth. The questions that camp raises in this context are, *Whose truth should be privileged? Whose narrative of the city is the true one? Where can we locate the truth about sex in the city?* Sinclair and Home both enjoy playing with the distinction between truth and fiction, as well as forging links between materiality of space and the impossibility of truth—by straining to locate a truth of the materiality of London (one produced out of the fragments, the decayed, the rejected). There are clear links here to camp, once described by the gay artist Philip Core as "the lie that tells the truth" (1985). These two writers, although not self-consciously camp, are doing the same work that camp does in reclaiming the lost value of objects and spaces and revalorizing things and places. Sinclair admires Home's attention to trash, writing that he "trashes trash—to grant it a second life. He models his prose style on non-prose, tabloid journalism: that hybrid of pictograph and scored shriek. Speed is everything" (1997, 224).

"A Wanker Is a Wanker"

Despite his obvious enthusiasm for Home's psychogeographical *detournement* of the truth and the authentic experience of place, Sinclair is quick to castigate Home's skinheadism—the embodiment of Home's defiance against notions of authenticity. He is quick to point toward the evidence of the fascist British National Party (BNP) election victory on the Isle of Dogs in 1994 as proof that Home may be at best misguided in his psychogeographical excursions around the East End:

> South of Teviot the game gets darker, you're closing on Dog Island, the remnant overshadowed by the vanity of Canary Wharf: the end zone targeted by Derek Beacon and his lumpen followers in the BNP. This is where Home enters into a ludic contract with the demonology of the skinhead. Dangerous games: on the estate, he's been pelted with stones. The unsophisticated proles haven't managed to keep abreast of the latest recyclings from the Frankfurt School. If you skulk around in small-check Ben Shermans, slippery bomber jacket, Doc Martens, with a No. 1 crop glossing towards suedehead, then you *are* what you appear to be. They haven't grasped the niceties of role playing, gender jumping, street theatre. A wanker is a wanker. And he's soliciting a thorough-going, ironically anachronistic kicking. (1997, 223)

The term *unsophisticated proles* is Sinclair's, not Home's. Sinclair implies that these "proles" are not the arbiters of street fashion—they cannot read the signs and symbols of the street. He suggests that the elite are the arbiters of street fashion; they are the ones that lead and interpret street fashion. In London in the 1990s, you are more likely to be given an "ironically anachronistic kicking" for being a poof wearing small-check Ben Shermans. In the late 1990s, Ben Shermans have become fashionable on the High Street among straight lads. The cycle of (straight) appropriation and (queer) reappropriation means that it is far too simplistic for Sinclair to argue that "you *are* what you appear to be." Maybe the only "wanker" here is Sinclair himself?

Sinclair quotes freely from Stewart Home's *Red London, Defiant Pose,* and *No Pity.* They are works where polymorphous perversity is central to the action. Earlier in this chapter, I traced the polymorphous perversity of Home's truth about sex in the city. However, when Sinclair discusses sexuality in Home's writing on London, there appears to be little that is polymorphously perverse. Sinclair describes Home's erotic city in blatantly heterosexual, gendered language, especially when he writes that London is Home's "bitch and his bride" (1997, 226). He also asserts that by making explicit the links between eroticism and urbanism, Home is somehow dirty, perverse, and, worst of all, sexually frustrated, and that Home is "hot to fuck the city. But he is as frustrated as one of Bunuel's lecherous old dons, he can't find a centre" (225). So it seems that Sinclair uses Home's writing to bolster the stability and authenticity of his own position as a commentator on the perverse, nether-reaches of the imperial capital.

Having discussed the materiality of sex in the city via Home and Sinclair, I now want to widen my focus to reevaluate links between the production and representation of (sexualized) bodies and the urban space—a core theme of this chapter that, I have argued, has been neglected in the emerging geographical literature on sexuality and space.

Representing Sexuality and Urban Space

Concluding this chapter, I want to examine—in light of my discussion of the articulation and production of bodies and spaces in the novels of Stewart Home (and in Sinclair's commentaries on Home)—what is unique about the relationship between the production of spaces and bodies in queer SM: What can this relationship tell us about the production of sexualities and cities?

The bodies in Stewart Home's novels occupy the margins—the discarded remnants of the city. The staging of these particular bodies in these spaces challenges the meanings of both bodies and spaces. Whose queer imaginary is being constructed through Home's novels? How can we trace the queerness in these images? Home's and his protagonists' assertion of an "in-your-face" attitude demonstrates the assertion of a right to be different from the norm. As Michael Bronski has argued, "the blatant public image of the leather man (or woman) is an outright threat to the . . . system of gender arrangements and sexual repression under which we have all lived" (1991, 64). Queer citizenship resides in being able to read Home's texts as contributing toward an *urban queer aesthetic*. But, as with any formation of citizenship, membership of a community is predicated on exclusion. Those who are excluded from this particular queer citizenship are those who fail to read queer desire into these texts.

What is most salient about Stewart Home's work is that in them it is much easier to articulate how cities are sexualized—how urban space is eroticized in fiction—than it is in conventional academic discourse. Fiction comes much closer to establishing a "truth" about sexuality in the city than academic writing on the subject has to date. Iain Sinclair bolsters his authority as a narrator of the perverse by referring to Home's writings— thereby representing the polymorphously perverse in a distanced manner. His treatment of Home boosts his own authenticity as urban narrator as well as the fixity and rigidity of gender identity. Although Sinclair articulates an element of eroticism in his urban narrative, this articulation is carefully managed and limited to a celebration of the perverse Other from the position of a stable subject. Here it may be appropriate to quote from Edmund White's *States of Desire,* where White argues that we must be aware of the will to hypocrisy that narrative power provides: "It strikes me that a kind of hypocrisy is so prevalent as to be almost undetectable: the habit of castigating in print what one accepts, even enjoys, in life. I feel the temptation myself to pass judgement in this essay on those situations that I ramble through once a month without a thought. Is it because language belongs to the oppressor?" (1986, 284).

In *The Body of This Death,* William Haver provides an elegant and enthusiastic discussion of Sue Golding's performative work on SM. However, despite her brilliance and charm, he expresses some ambivalence about her deployment of tit clamps and the paraphernalia of SM in discourse, noting that

> Golding's rhetorical address stages, paradoxically to be sure, the recognition scene of an intersubjective interpretative community within which intelligibility and sense are precisely what goes without saying. For those of us for whom tit clamps, cuffs, rope, and so on are indeed among the instruments of play, the assurance of mutual understanding would be quite beside the point; *to suggest that something goes without saying can only mean that it does in fact need saying.* (1996, 187, my emphasis)

    I sometimes experience a certain discomfort when I read some ac-
counts of public sex and SM in academic texts. This discomfort is not the
squeamishness associated with queer sex, but rather an uneasiness about
the distanced representations of it. For whom are these acts, these spaces,
being made intellgible? What is the point? To phrase it in Haver's dense
language, for which "interpretative subjective community" are these accounts being produced? This is not to deny the validity of inserting accounts of queer sex into discourse. It is more that there are questions about
representation that we need to consider in our work on sexuality and
space. These issues are particularly pressing in the classroom, as a number
of writers are now arguing. In her essay "Queer and Now," Eve Sedgwick
(1994) admits to having nightmares about designing courses on lesbian
and gay studies: Who are these courses for? She complains of her straight-
defined students' sense of entitlement to have every aspect of dissident
sexualities explained to them, made readily understandable to them,
whereas other highly expectant queer students in the class have invested
their whole identity and survival in the class. The question of representation, then, is one we all must consider in our teaching and in our writing.
Texts, like bodies and spaces, are read as well as written, and the production of urban queer space and embodiment is always matched by its consumption, which can be ambivalent. As we see in Sinclair's downplaying
of Home's queer fictions and in the commodification of urban queer space,
readers can skip those parts of the text they don't want to deal with.

References
Index

References

Adler, Sy, and Joanna Brenner. 1992. "Gender and Space: Lesbians and Gays in the City." *International Journal of Urban and Regional Research* 16, no. 1: 24–34.

Ainley, Rosa. 1995. *What Is She Like?: Lesbian Identities from the 1950s to the 1990s*. London: Cassell.

———. 1998. *New Frontiers of Space, Bodies, and Gender*. London: Routledge.

Allen, Richard. 1992. *Skinhead*. Dunoon: ST.

Anderson, Kay. 1996. "Engendering Race Research: Unsettling the Self-Other Dichotomy." In *Body Space*, edited by Nancy Duncan, 197–211. London and New York: Routledge.

Appadurai, Arjun. 1990. "Disjuncture and Difference in the Global Cultural Economy." In *Global Culture: Nationalism, Globalization, and Modernity*, edited by Mike Featherstone, 295–310. London: Sage.

Bachelard, Gaston. 1969. *The Poetics of Space*. Boston: Beacon.

Barnard, Malcolm. 1996. *Fashion As Communication*. London: Routledge.

Baudrillard, Jean. 1983. *In the Shadow of the Silent Majorities*. New York: Semotext(e).

———. 1992. "Jean Baudrillard from *Simulations*." In *A Critical and Cultural Theory Reader*, edited by E. A. Easthope and K. McGowan, 203–5. Sydney: Allen and Unwin.

Bech, Henning. 1997. *When Men Meet: Homosexuality and Modernity*. Cambridge: Polity.

Bell, David. 1991. "Insignificant Others: Lesbian and Gay Geographies." *Area* 23, no. 4: 323–29.

———. 1995a. "Perverse Dynamics, Sexual Citizenship, and the Transformation of Intimacy." In *Mapping Desire: Geographies of Sexualities*, edited by David Bell and Gill Valentine, 304–17. London: Routledge.

———. 1995b. "[*Screw*]ing Geography: Censor's Version." *Environment and Planning D: Society and Space* 13: 127–32.

———. 1996. Review of *Foreign Bodies*, by Alphonso Lingis, and *Sensuous Geographies*, by Paul Rodaway. *Environment and Planning D: Society and Space* 14: 621–23.

Bell, David, and Jon Binnie. 1996. "Sexual Cultures in Europe: Geographical Perspectives." Paper presented at the Sexual Cultures in Europe Conference, June, Amsterdam.

———. 1998. "Theatres of Cruelty, Rivers of Desire: The Erotics of the Street." In *Images of the Street: Planning, Identity, and Control in Public Space,* edited by Nicholas R. Fyfe, 129–40. London: Routledge.

———. 2000. *The Sexual Citizen: Queer Politics and Beyond.* Cambridge: Polity.

Bell, David, Jon Binnie, Julia Cream, and Gill Valentine. 1994. "All Hyped Up and No Place to Go." *Gender, Place, and Culture* 1: 31–48.

Bell, David, and Gill Valentine. 1995a. "Introduction: Orientations." In *Mapping Desire: Geographies of Sexualities,* edited by David Bell and Gill Valentine, 1–27. London: Routledge.

———, eds. 1995b. *Mapping Desire: Geographies of Sexualities.* London: Routledge.

———. 1995c. "Queer Country: Rural Lesbian and Gay Lives." *Journal of Rural Studies* 11: 113–22.

———. 1995d. "The Sexed Self: Strategies of Performance, Sites of Resistance." In *Mapping the Subject: Geographies of Cultural Transformation,* edited by Steve Pile and Nigel Thrift, 143–57. London: Routledge.

———. 1997. *Consuming Geographies: We Are Where We Eat.* London: Routledge.

Berg, Larry, and Robin Kearns. 1998. "American Unlimited." *Environment and Planning D: Society and Space* 18: 128–32.

Berlant, Lauren. 1997. *The Queen of America Goes to Washington City: Essays on Sex and Citizenship.* Durham, N.C.: Duke Univ. Press.

Beyer, J. 1992. "Sexual Minorities and Geography." Paper presented at the Twenty-Seventh International Geographical Congress, August, Washington, D.C.

Bhabha, Homi. 1994. *The Location of Culture.* London: Routledge.

Binnie, Jon. 1995a. "Trading Places: Consumption, Sexuality, and the Production of Queer Space." In *Mapping Desire: Geographies of Sexualities,* edited by David Bell and Gill Valentine, 182–99. London: Routledge.

———. 1995b. "The Trouble with Camp." *Transgressions: A Journal of Urban Exploration* 1: 51–58.

———. 1997a. "Coming Out of Geography: Notes Towards a Queer Epistemology." *Environment and Planning D: Society and Space* 15: 223–37.

———. 1997b. "Invisible Europeans: Sexual Citizenship in the New Europe." *Environment and Planning A* 29: 237–48.

Binnie, Jon, and Gill Valentine. 1999. "Geographies of Sexuality: A Review of Progress." *Progress in Human Geography* 23: 175–87.

Blank, R. H. 1992. *Mother and Fetus: Changing Notions of Maternal Responsibility.* Contributions in Medical Studies, no. 36. New York: Greenwood.

Boffin, Tessa, and Jean Fraser. 1990. *Stolen Glances: Lesbians Take Photographs.* London: Pandora.

Bondi, Liz. 1990. "Progress in Geography and Gender: Feminism and Difference." *Progress in Human Geography* 14, no. 3: 438–45.

———. 1992. "Sexing the City." Paper presented at the Association of American Geographers Annual Conference, March, San Diego.

———. 1993. "Locating Identity Politics." In *Place and the Politics of Identity,* edited by Michael Keith and Steve Pile, 84–101. London and New York: Routledge.

Brah, Avtar. 1996. *Cartographies of Diaspora: Contesting Identities.* London and New York: Routledge.

Bredbeck, Gregory W. 1996. "Troping the Light Fantastic: Representing Disco Then and Now." *GLQ* 3: 71–107.

Brent-Ingram, Gordon, Anne Marie Bouthilette, and Yolanda Retter, eds. 1997. *Queers in Space: Communities, Public Places, Sites of Resistance.* Seattle: Bay.

Bronski. Michael. 1991. "A Dream Is a Wish Your Heart Makes: Notes on the Materialization of Sexual Fantasy." In *Leatherfolk: Radical Sex, People, Politics, and Practice,* edited by Mark Thompson, 56–64. Boston, Mass.: Alyson.

Brown, Michael. 1995. "Sex, Scale, and the 'New Urban Politics': HIV-Prevention Strategies from Yaletown, Vancouver." In *Mapping Desire: Geographies of Sexualities,* edited by David Bell and Gill Valentine, 245–63. London: Routledge.

Brunn, S. D. 1992. "Are We Missing Our Forests for Our Trees? It's Time for a Census." *Annals of the Association of American Geographers* 82, no. 1: 1–2.

Butler, Judith. 1990. *Gender Trouble: Feminism and the Subversion of Identity.* London: Routledge.

———. 1991. "Imitation and Gender Insubordination." In *Inside/Out,* edited by Diana Fuss, 13–31. New York: Routledge.

———. 1993. *Bodies That Matter: On the Discursive Limits of "Sex."* London: Routledge.

———. 1997. *Excitable Speech: A Politics of the Performative.* New York: Routledge.

Califia, Pat. 1994. *Public Sex: The Culture of Radical Sex.* Pittsburgh: Cleis.

———. 1997. "San Francisco: Revisiting 'The City of Desire.' " In *Queers in Space: Communities, Public Places, Sites of Resistance,* edited by Gordon Brent-Ingram, Anne-Marie Bouthillette, and Yolanda Retter, 177–96. Seattle: Bay.

Campbell, Colin. 1995. "The Sociology of Consumption." In *Acknowledging Consumption,* edited by Daniel Miller, 96–126. London: Routledge.

———. 1996. "The Meaning of Objects and the Meaning of Actions." *Journal of Material Culture,* 1, no. 1: 93–105.

Castells, Manuel. 1977. *The Urban Question: A Marxist Approach.* Translated by A. Sheridan. London: Edward Arnold.

———. 1983. *The City and the Grassroots.* Berkeley, Calif.: Univ. of California Press.

Census of Population and Dwellings. 1996. *National Summary.* Wellington: Department of Statistics.

Chambers, I., and L. Curti, eds. 1996. *The Postcolonial Question: Common Skies, Divided Horizons.* London and New York: Routledge.

Champion, L., and M. O'Neill. 1993. "Exercise and Pregnancy." *Network* (June-July): 29–33.

Chauncey, George. 1996. " 'Privacy Could Only Be Had in Public': Gay Uses of the Streets." In *Stud: Architectures of Masculinity,* edited by Joel Sanders, 224–67. New York: Princeton Architectural Press.

Chouinard, Vera, and Ali Grant. 1996. "On Not Being Anywhere Near 'The Project': Ways of Putting Ourselves in the Picture." In *BodySpace,* edited by Nancy Duncan, 170–93. London and New York: Routledge.

Chtcheglov, I. 1981. "Formulary for a New Urbanism." In *Situationist International Anthology,* edited and translated by K. Knabb, 1–4. Berkeley, Calif.: Bureau of Public Secrets.

Cohan, Steven. 1996. "So Functional for Its Purposes: Rock Hudson's Bachelor Apartment in *Pillow Talk.*" In *Stud: Architectures of Masculinity,* edited by Joel Sanders, 28–41. New York: Princeton Architectural Press.

Cole, C. L. 1994. "Resisting the Canon: Feminist Cultural Studies, Sport, and Technologies of the Body." In *Women, Sport, and Culture,* edited by S. Birrell and C. L. Cole, 52–74. Champaign, Ill.: Human Kinetics.

Colomina, Beatriz, ed. 1992. *Sexuality and Space.* New York: Princeton Architectural Press.

Constant. 1997. "A Different City for a Different Life." *October* 79: 109–12. (Originally published in *Internationale Situationniste* 3 [1959].)

Cook, G. 1990. "Transcribing Infinity: Problems of Context Presentation." *Journal of Pragmatics* 14: 1–24.

Core, Philip. 1985. *Camp: The Lie That Tells the Truth.* New York: Delilah.

Cornwell, J. 1993. "Carry on Class War." *i-D* 122: 105–6.

Corzine, J., and R. Kirby. 1977. "Cruising the Truckers: Sexual Encounters in a Highway Rest Area." *Urban Life* 6: 171–92.

Crawford, S. 1987. " 'One's Nerves and Courage Are in Very Different Order Out in New Zealand': Recreational and Sporting Opportunities for Women in a Remote Colonial Setting." In *From 'Fair Sex' to Feminism,* edited by J. A. Mangan and R. J. Park, 63–81. London: Frank Cass.

Cream, Julia. 1995. "Re-solving Riddles: The Sexed Body." In *Mapping Desire: Geographies of Sexualities,* edited by David Bell and Gill Valentine, 31–40. London: Routledge.

Crimp, Douglas. 1993a. "On the Museum's Ruins." In *On The Museum's Ruins,* 44–64. Cambridge, Mass.: MIT Press.

———. 1993b. "Photographs at the End of Modernism." In *On the Museum's Ruins,* 2–41. Cambridge, Mass.: MIT Press.

Crimp, Douglas, and Adam Rolston. 1990. *AIDS Demo Graphics.* Seattle: Bay.

Currah, Paisley. 1995. "Searching for Immutability: Homosexuality, Race, and Rights Discourse." In *A Simple Matter of Justice?: Theorizing Lesbian and Gay Politics*, edited by Angelia Wilson, 91–109. London: Cassell.

Currid, Brian. 1995. " 'We Are Family': House Music and Queer Performativity." In *Cruising the Performative: Interventions into the Representation of Ethnicity, Nationality, and Sexuality*, edited by Sue-Ellen Case, Philip Brett, and Susan Foster, 165–96. Bloomington, Ind.: Indiana Univ. Press.

Davis, Tim. 1995. "The Diversity of Sexual Politics and the Redefinition of Sexual Identity and Community in Urban Spaces." In *Mapping Desire: Geographies of Sexualities*, edited by David Bell and Gill Valentine, 284–303. London: Routledge.

Debord, Guy. 1981. "Theory of the Dérive." In *Situationist International Anthology*, edited and translated by K. Knabb, 50–54. Berkeley, Calif.: Bureau of Public Secrets.

de Certeau, Michel. 1984. *The Practice of Everyday Life*. Berkeley, Calif.: Univ. of California Press.

Delany, Samuel. 1995. "Aversion/Perversion/Diversion." In *Negotiating Lesbian and Gay Subjectivities*, edited by Monica Dorenkamp and Richard Henke, 7–33. London: Routledge.

Dellamora, Richard. 1990. *Masculine Desire: The Sexual Politics of Victorian Aestheticism*. Chapel Hill: Univ. of North Carolina Press.

Dorn, Michael, and Glenda Laws. 1994. "Social Theory, Body Politics, and Medical Geography: Extending Kearns's Invitation." *Professional Geographer* 46: 106–10.

Douglas, Mary. 1966. *Purity and Danger*. London: Routledge and Kegan Paul.

Douglas, M., and B. Isherwood. 1996. *The World of Goods: Towards an Anthropology of Consumption* (with a new introduction). London and New York: Routledge.

Duggan, Lisa. 1995a. "The Discipline Problem: Queer Theory Meets Lesbian and Gay History." *GLQ* 2: 179–91.

———. 1995b. "Queering the State." In *Sex Wars*, edited by Lisa Duggan and Nan Hunter, 179–93. New York: Routledge.

Duncan, Nancy. 1996. "Renegotiating Gender and Sexuality in Public and Private Spaces." In *BodySpace*, edited by Nancy Duncan, 127–45. London and New York: Routledge.

Dunden, B. 1991. *The Woman Beneath the Skin: A Doctor's Patients in Eighteenth Century Germany*. Translated by T. Dunlap. Boston, Mass.: Harvard Univ. Press.

Dyck, I. 1995. "Hidden Geographies: The Changing Lifeworlds of Women with Multiple Sclerosis." *Social Science and Medicine* 40, no. 3: 307–20.

Dyer, Richard. 1992. "In Defence of Disco." In *Only Entertainment*, 149–58. London: Routledge.

Eadie, Jo. 1992. "The Motley Crew: What's at Stake in the Production of Bisexual

Identity." Paper presented at the Sexuality and Space Network Conference, "Lesbian and Gay Geographies?" September, London.

Easthope, E. A., and K. McGowan, eds. 1992. *A Critical and Cultural Theory Reader.* Sydney: Allen and Unwin.

Edelman, Lee. 1992. "Tearooms and Sympathy, or, The Epistemology of the Water Closet." In *Nationalisms and Sexualities,* edited by Andrew Parker, Mary Russo, Doris Sommer, and Patricia Yaeger, 263–84. London: Routledge.

———. 1994. *Homographesis: Essays in Gay Literary and Cultural Theory.* New York: Routledge.

Fone, B. 1983. "This Other Eden: Arcadia and the Homosexual Imagination." *Journal of Homosexuality* 8: 13–34.

Foucault, Michel. 1977. *Discipline and Punish: The Birth of the Prison.* Translated by A. Sheridan. London: Penguin.

———. 1980. *The History of Sexuality.* Vol. 1, *An Introduction.* Translated by R. Hurley. New York: Vintage, Random House.

———. 1985. *The History of Sexuality.* Vol. 2, *The Use of Pleasure.* Translated by R. Hurley. New York: Pantheon.

———. 1986. *The History of Sexuality.* Vol. 3, *The Care of the Self.* Translated by R. Hurley. New York: Pantheon.

Frank, Marcie. 1993. "The Critic as Performance Artist: Susan Sontag's Writing and Gay Cultures." In *Camp Grounds: Style and Homosexuality,* edited by David Bergman, 173–84. Amherst, Mass.: Univ. of Massachusetts Press.

Fraser, Mariam. 1997. "Lose Your Face." In *The Bisexual Imaginary: Representation, Identity, and Desire,* edited by Bi Academic Intervention, 38–57. London: Cassell.

Freud, Sigmund. 1914. "On Narcissism: An Introduction." In *Standard Edition of the Complete Psychological Works of Sigmund Freud,* edited and translated by J. Strachey, 14:213–36. London: Hogarth.

Frye, Marilyn. 1983. *The Politics of Reality: Essays in Feminist Theory.* Freedom, Calif.: Crossing.

———. 1985. "History and Responsibility." *Hypatia: Women's Studies International Forum* 8, no. 3: 215–17.

———. 1992. *Wilful Virgin: Essays in Feminism.* Freedom, Calif.: Crossing.

Fuss, Diane. 1989. *Essentially Speaking: Feminism, Nature, and Difference.* London: Routledge.

———, ed. 1991. *Inside Out: Lesbian Theories, Gay Theories.* New York: Routledge.

Gallagher, C., and T. Laqueur. 1987. *The Making of the Modern Body.* Berkeley, Calif.: Univ. of California Press.

Gardner, C. B. 1994. "The Social Construction of Pregnancy and Fetal Development: Notes on a Nineteenth-Century Rhetoric of Endangerment." In *Con-*

structing the Social, edited by T. R. Sarbin and J. I. Kitsuse, 141–54. London: Sage.

Gatens, Moira. 1992. "Power, Bodies, and Difference." In *Destabilizing Theory: Contemporary Feminist Debates,* edited by M. Barrett and A. Phillips, 120–37. Cambridge: Polity.

———. 1996. *Imaginary Bodies: Ethics, Power, and Corporeality.* London: Routledge.

Geltmaker, Ty. 1992. "The Queer Nation Acts Up: Health Care, Politics, and Sexual Diversity in the County of Angels." *Environment and Planning D: Society and Space* 10: 609–50.

Gerber, E., ed. 1972. *Sport and the Body: A Philosophical Symposium.* Philadelphia.: Lea and Febiger.

Goffman, Erving. 1959. *The Presentation of the Self in Everyday Life.* Harmondsworth: Penguin.

Golding, Sue. 1993a. "The Excess: An Added Remark on Sex, Rubber, Ethics, and Other Impurities." *New Formations* 19: 23–28.

———. 1993b. "Quantum Philosophy, Impossible Geographies, and a Few Small Points about Life, Liberty, and the Pursuit of Sex (All in the Name of Democracy)." In *Place and the Politics of Identity,* edited by Michael Keith and Steve Pile, 206–19. London: Routledge.

———. 1993c. "Sexual Manners." In *Pleasure Principles: Politics, Sexuality, and Ethics,* edited by V. Harwood, D. Oswell, K. Parkinson, and A. Ward, 80–89. London: Lawrence and Wishart.

———. 1997. "The Delicate Web of Subversion, Friendship, and Love." In *The Eight Technologies of Otherness,* edited by Sue Golding, 320–33. London and New York: Routledge.

Graham, Paula. 1995. "Girl's Camp? The Politics of Parody." In *Immortal Invisible: Lesbians and the Moving Image,* edited by Tamsin Wilton, 163–81. London: Routledge.

Gregory, Derek, Ron Martin, and G. Smith. 1994. *Human Geography: Society, Space, and Social Science.* Houndmills: Macmillan.

Grosz, Elizabeth. 1989a. "Julia Kristeva: Abjection, Motherhood, and Love." In *Sexual Subversions: Three French Feminists,* 70–99. Sydney: Allen and Unwin.

———. 1989b. *Sexual Subversions: Three French Feminists.* Sydney: Allen and Unwin.

———. 1994. *Volatile Bodies: Toward a Corporeal Feminism.* Bloomington: Indiana Univ. Press.

———. 1995. *Space, Time, and Perversion.* St. Leonards: Allen and Unwin.

Grosz, Elizabeth, and Elspeth Probyn, eds. 1995. *Sexy Bodies: The Strange Carnalities of Feminism.* London and New York: Routledge.

Hall, Stuart. 1996. "Who Needs Identity?" In *Questions of Cultural Identity,* edited by Stuart Hall and Paul du Gay, 1–17. London: Sage.

Hallam, Paul. 1993. *The Book of Sodom*. London: Verso.

Hanson, F. A. 1982. "Female Pollution in Polynesia?" *Journal of Polynesian Society* 91, no. 1: 335–81.

Haraway, Donna. 1988. "Situated Knowledges: The Science Question in Feminism and the Privilege of the Partial Perspective." *Feminist Review* 14, no. 3: 575–99.

Harding, Sandra. 1991. *The Science Question in Feminism*. Milton Keynes: Open Univ. Press.

Harman, L. D. 1987. *The Modern Stranger: On Language and Membership*. Berlin: Mouton de Gruyter.

Harrison, M. R., N. S. Adzick, and M. Longaker. 1990. "Successful Repair in Utero of Fetal Diaphragmatic Hernia After Removal of Herniated Viscera from the Left Thorax." *New England Journal of Medicine* 322, no. 22: 1582–84.

Hartley, John. 1997. "The Sexualization of Suburbia: The Diffusion of Knowledge in the Postmodern Public Sphere." In *Visions of Suburbia*, edited by R. Silverstone, 180–216. London: Routledge.

Haver, William. 1996. *The Body of This Death: Historicity and Sociality in the Time of AIDS*. Stanford, Calif.: Stanford Univ. Press.

Hayden, Dolores. 1980. "What Would a Non-sexist City Be Like?" *Signs* 5: 170–87.

Healy, Murray. 1996. *Gay Skins: Class, Masculinity, and Queer Appropriation*. London: Cassell.

Hegarty, Peter. 1997. "Materializing the Hypothalamus: A Performative Account of the 'Gay Brain.' " *Feminism and Psychology* 7: 355–72.

Hepburn, L. 1992. *Ova-dose? Australian Women and the New Reproductive Technology*. Sydney: Allen and Unwin.

Hesse, Barnor. 1993. "Black to Front and Black Again: Racialization Through Contested Times and Spaces." In *Place and the Politics of Identity*, edited by Michael Keith and Steve Pile, 162–82. London and New York: Routledge.

Holliday, Ruth, and John Hassard, eds. 2001. *Contested Bodies*. London: Routledge.

Home, Stewart. 1989. *Pure Mania*. Edinburgh: Polygon.

———. 1991. *Defiant Pose*. London: Peter Owen.

———. 1993. *No Pity*. Edinburgh: AK.

———. 1994. *Red London*. Edinburgh: AK.

———. 1996. *Slow Death*. London: Serpent's Tail.

Humphries, Laud. 1970. *Tearoom Trade: Impersonal Sex in Public Places*. Chicago: Aldine.

Hunt, Leon. 1998. *British Low Culture: From Safari Suits to Sexploitation*. London: Routledge.

Jackson, Peter, ed. 1987. *Race and Racism*. London: Unwin Hyman.

———. 1989. *Maps of Meaning: An Introduction to Cultural Geography*. London: Unwin Hyman.

139

————. 1994. "Black Male: Advertising and the Cultural Politics of Masculinity." *Gender Place and Culture: A Journal of Feminist Geography* 1, no. 1: 49–60.

Jackson, Peter, and Susan J. Smith. 1984. *Social Interaction and Ethnic Segregation.* London: Academic.

Johnson, Louise. 1989. "Embodying Geography: Some Implications of Considering the Sexed Body in Space." In *New Zealand Geographical Society Proceedings of the 15th New Zealand Geography Conference*, 134–38. Dunedin: NZGS.

Johnston, Lynda. 1996. " 'Flexing Femininity': Female Body-Builders Refiguring 'the Body.' " *Gender, Place, and Culture: A Journal of Feminist Geography* 3, no. 3: 327–40.

Johnston, Lynda, and Gill Valentine. 1995. "Wherever I Lay My Girlfriend, That's My Home: The Performance and Surveillance of Lesbian Identities in Domestic Environments." In *Mapping Desire: Geographies of Sexualities*, edited by David Bell and Gill Valentine, 99–113. London: Routledge.

Johnston, Ron J. 1991. *A Question of Place: Exploring the Practice of Human Geography.* Oxford: Blackwell.

Keith, Michael, and Steve Pile, eds. 1993. *Place and the Politics of Identity.* London and New York: Routledge.

Kenney, J. W., and D. T. Tash. 1993. "Lesbian Childbearing Dilemmas and Decisions." In *Lesbian Health: What Are the Issues?* edited by P. Noerager Stern, 120–42. Washington, D.C.: Taylor and Francis.

Kirby, K. 1996. "Re:mapping Subjectivity: Cartographic Vision and the Limits of Politics." In *BodySpace*, edited by Nancy Duncan, 45–55. London and New York: Routledge.

Knopp, Lawrence. 1987. "Social Theory, Social Movements, and Public Policy: Recent Accomplishments of the Gay and Lesbian Movements in Minneapolis, Minnesota." *International Journal of Urban and Regional Research* 11: 243–61.

————. 1990a. "Exploiting the Rent-Gap: The Theoretical Significance of Using Illegal Appraisal Schemes to Encourage Gentrification in New Orleans." *Urban Geography* 11: 48–64.

————. 1990b. "Some Theoretical Implications of Gay Involvement in an Urban Land Market." *Political Geography Quarterly* 9: 337–52.

————. 1995. "Sexuality and Urban Space: A Framework for Analysis." In *Mapping Desire: Geographies of Sexualities*, edited by David Bell and Gill Valentine, 149–61. London: Routledge.

Kramer, Jerry Lee. 1995. "Bachelor Farmers and Spinsters: Gay and Lesbian Identities and Communities in Rural North Dakota." In *Mapping Desire: Geographies of Sexualities*, edited by David Bell and Gill Valentine, 200–213. London: Routledge.

Kristeva, Julia. 1982. *Powers of Horror: An Essay on Abjection.* Translated by L. S. Roudiez. New York: Columbia Univ. Press.

———. 1991. *Strangers to Ourselves.* Translated by L. S. Roudiez. New York: Columbia Univ. Press.

Kureshi, Hanif. 1990. *The Buddha of Suburbia.* London: Faber and Faber.

Laqueur, T. 1990. *Making Sex: Body and Gender from the Greeks to Freud.* London: Harvard Univ. Press.

Larner, W., and P. Spoonley. Forthcoming. "Postcolonial Politics in Aotearoa/New Zealand." In *Gender, Race, Ethnicity, and Class in Settler Colonies: Against Dichotomies,* edited by D. Stasiulis and Nira Yuval-Davis. London: Sage.

Lee, John Alan. 1983. "The Social Organization of Risk." In *S & M: Studies in Sadomasochism,* edited by Thomas S. Weinberg and G. W. Levi Kamel, 175–93. Buffalo, N.Y.: Prometheus.

Lefort, C. 1996. "Sade: The Boudoir and the City." *South Atlantic Quarterly* 95: 1009–28.

Lewis, Reina, and Katrina Rolley. 1997. "(Ad)ressing the Dyke: Lesbian Looks and Lesbians Looking." In *Buy This Book: Studies in Advertising and Consumption,* edited by M. Nava, A. Blake, I. MacRury, and B. Richards, 291–308. London: Routledge.

Lieshout, Maurice van. 1995. "Leather Nights in the Woods: Homosexual Encounters in a Dutch Highway Rest Area." *Journal of Homosexuality* 29: 19–39.

Lingis, Alphonso. 1994. *Foreign Bodies.* New York: Routledge.

Listener. 1995. "Who Is Left Holding the Baby?" January 21, 14–15.

Longhurst, Robyn. 1997. "(Dis)embodied Geographies." *Progress in Human Geography* 21: 486–501.

———. 2001. *Bodies: Exploring Fluid Boundaries* London: Routledge.

Longhurst, Robyn, and Lynda Johnston. Forthcoming. "Embodying Places and Emplacing Bodies: Pregnant Women and Women Body Builders." In *Crafting Connections/Defining Differences,* edited by R. Du Plessis and L. Alice. Oxford: Oxford Univ. Press.

Lurie, Alison. 1981. *The Language of Clothes.* New York: Random House.

Lynch, F. 1992. "Nonghetto Gays: An Ethnography of Suburban Homosexuals." In *Gay Culture in America: Essays from the Field,* edited by Gilbert Herdt, 165–201. Boston: Beacon.

MacClancy, Jeremy. 1993. *Consuming Culture: Why You Eat What You Eat.* New York: Henry Holt.

Mains, Geoff. 1984. *Urban Aboriginals: A Celebration of Leathersexuality.* San Francisco: Gay Sunshine.

Marshall, George. 1991. *Spirit of '69: A Skinhead Bible.* Dunoon, Scotland: ST.

Martin, Biddy. 1993. "Lesbian Identity and Autobiographical Difference(s)." In *The Lesbian and Gay Studies Reader,* edited by Henry Abelove, Michele Aina Barale, and David M. Halperin, 274–93. London: Routledge.

Maynard, Stephen. 1999. " 'Respect Your Elders, Know Your Past': History and the Queer Theorists." *Radical History Review* 75: 56–78.

McDowell, Linda. 1991. "The Baby and the Bath Water: Diversity, Deconstruction, and Feminist Theory in Geography." *Geoforum* 22, no. 2: 123–33.

———. 1995. "Body Work: Heterosexual Gender Performances in City Workplaces." In *Mapping Desire: Geographies of Sexualities,* edited by David Bell and Gill Valentine, 75–95. London: Routledge.

———. 1996. "Spatializing Feminism: Geographic Perspectives." In *BodySpace,* edited by Nancy Duncan, 28–44. London and New York: Routledge.

———. 1997. *Capital Culture: Money, Sex, and Power at Work.* Oxford: Blackwell.

McDowell, Linda, and Joan Sharp, eds. 1999. *A Feminist Glossary of Human Geography.* London: Arnold.

Middleton, J. 1996. "Life and Death Struggles." *Listener,* February 10, 18–22.

Mitchell, William. 1995. *City of Bits: Space, Place, and the Infobahn.* Cambridge, Mass.: MIT Press.

Mittelmark, R. A., R. Wisswell, and B. L. Drinkwater, eds. 1991. *Exercise in Pregnancy.* Sydney: Williams and Wilkins.

Moore, Clive. 1995. "Poofs in the Park: Documenting Gay 'Beats' in Queensland, Australia." *GLQ* 2: 319–39.

Moos, Adam. 1989. "The Grassroots in Action: Gays and Seniors Capture the Local State in West Hollywood, California." In *The Power of Geography: How Territory Shapes Social Life,* edited by Jennifer Wolch and Michael Dear, 67–93. Boston: Unwin Hyman.

Moran, Leslie J. 1995. "Violence and the Law: The Case of Sado-masochism." *Social and Legal Studies* 4: 225–51.

———. 1996. *The Homosexual(ity) of Law.* London: Routledge.

Morgan, D. H. J., and S. Scott. 1993. "Bodies in a Social Landscape." In *Body Matters,* edited by S. Scott and D. H. J. Morgan, 1–21. London: Falmer.

Morgan, W. J., and K. V. Meier, eds. 1988. *Philosophic Inquiry in Sport.* Leeds: Human Kinetics.

Mort, Frank. 1997. "Paths to Mass Consumption: Britain and the USA Since 1945." In *Buy This Book: Studies in Advertising and Consumption,* edited by M. Nava, A. Blake, I. MacRury, and B. Richards, 15–33. London: Routledge.

Munt, Sally. 1995. "The Lesbian Flâneur." In *Mapping Desire: Geographies of Sexualities,* edited by David Bell and Gill Valentine, 114–25. London: Routledge.

———. 1996. "The Butch Body." Paper presented at the Body and Organization Workshop, September 12–13, Keele University.

Murray, Alison. 1995. "Femme on the Streets, Butch in the Sheets (a Play on Whores)." In *Mapping Desire: Geographies of Sexualities,* edited by David Bell and Gill Valentine, 66–74. London: Routledge.

Nast, Heidi J., and Steve Pile, eds. 1998. *Places Through the Body*. London: Routledge.

Nestle, Joan. 1987. *A Restricted Country: Essays and Short Stories*. London: Sheba.

New Spirit. 1994. "Joanna Paul: A Celebration of Life." August: 4–6.

New Zealand Obstetrical and Gynaecological Society. 1953. *The Expectant Mother*. Christchurch: Whitcombe and Tombs.

New Zealand Official 1996 Year Book, 99th ed. 1996. Auckland: Department of Statistics, Te Tari Tatau.

Nietzsche, Frederick. 1969. *On the Genealogy of Morals*. Translated by Walter Kaufmann and R. J. Hollingdale. New York: Vintage.

Nixon, Sean. 1996. *Hard Looks: Masculinities, the Visual, and Practices of Consumption*. London: UCL Press.

Ochs, E. 1979. "Transcription as Theory." In *Developmental Pragmatics*, edited by E. Ochs and B. Schieffelin, 32–46. New York: Academic.

Oliver, K. 1993. *Reading Kristeva: Unravelling the Double Bind*. Bloomington: Indiana Univ. Press.

Osius, A. 1993. "Godzilla Goes Climbing." *Climbing* (October-November): 166–68.

Oswell, D. 1996. "Suburbia, Sexual Hybridity, and the Troubles of Liberalism." Paper presented at the City Limits Conference, July, Staffordshire University.

———. n.d. " 'I'll Fuck Anybody': True Love in Queer Times." Unpublished paper.

Pateman, C. 1988. *The Sexual Contract*. Cambridge: Polity.

Patton, Paul, 1995. "Imaginary Cities: Images of Postmodernity." In *Postmodern Cities and Spaces*, edited by Sophie Watson and Kathy Gibson, 112–21. Oxford: Blackwell.

Peace, Robin. Forthcoming. *Ephemeral Identities: Problems and Possibilities in Lesbian Geography*. Department of Women's Studies Occasional Paper Series. Hamilton: University of Waikato.

———. n.d. "Queering the Patch—Occupation of Liminal Space: the Invisible/Visible Lesbian Other." Department of Geography, University of Waikato, Hamilton. Unpublished research project.

Perez-Gomez, Alberto. 1994. *Polyphilo or The Dark Forest Revisited: An Erotic Epiphany of Architecture*. Cambridge, Mass.: MIT Press.

Peterson, J. A. 1994. "Making Mama Fit: Exercise and the Pregnant Woman." *Muscular Development, Fitness, and Health* (June): 32 and 126.

Pfohl, Stephen. 1993. "Venus in Microsoft." In *The Last Sex: Feminism and Outlaw Bodies*, edited by Arthur Kroker and Marilouise Kroker, 184–97. Basingstoke: Macmillan.

Pickles, J. 1992. "Texts, Hermeneutics, and Propaganda Maps." In *Writing Worlds: Discourse, Text, and Metaphor in the Representation of Landscape*, edited by T. Barnes and J. Duncan, 193–230. London: Routledge.

Pile, Steve. 1996. *The Body in the City: Psychoanalysis, Space, and Subjectivity*. London: Routledge.

Pile, Steve, and Nigel Thrift. 1995. *Mapping the Subject: Geographies of Cultural Transformation.* London and New York: Routledge.

Pilgrim, J. n.d. "Language and Lack: Kiki Smith and Representation of the Naked Pregnant Body." Unpublished paper, University of Western Sydney, Nepean.

Plant, Sadie. 1992. *The Most Radical Gesture: The Situationist International in a Postmodern Age.* London: Routledge.

Polhemus, T., and H. Randall. 1994. *Rituals of Love: Sexual Experiments, Erotic Possibilities.* London: Picador.

Ponte, M. 1974. "Life in a Parking Lot: An Ethnography of a Homosexual Drive-in." In *Deviance: Field Studies and Self-disclosures,* edited by J. Jacobs, 7–29. Palo Alto, Calif.: National.

Probyn, Elspeth. 1993. *Sexing the Self: Gendered Positions in Cultural Studies.* London: Routledge.

———. 1995a. "Lesbians in Space: Gender, Sex, and the Structure of Missing." *Gender, Place, and Culture* 2, no. 1: 77–84.

———. 1995b. "Queer Belongings: The Politics of Departure." In *Sexy Bodies: The Strange Carnalities of Feminism,* edited by Elizabeth Grosz and Elspeth Probyn, 1–18. London: Routledge.

Raban, Jonathan. 1974. *Soft City.* London: Hamish Hamilton.

Rancière, J. 1992. "Politics, Identification, and Subjectivization." *October* 61: 58–65.

Rodaway, Paul. 1994. *Sensuous Geographies.* London: Routledge.

Rogers, A., H. Viles, and A. Goudie. 1992. *The Student's Companion to Geography.* Oxford: Blackwell.

Rose, Gillian. 1993. *Feminism and Geography.* Cambridge: Polity.

Rothenberg, Tamar. 1995. " 'And She Told Two Friends': Lesbians Creating Urban Social Space." In *Mapping Desire: Geographies of Sexualities,* edited by David Bell and Gill Valentine, 165–81. London: Routledge.

Rubin, Gayle. 1998. "The Miracle Mile: South of Market and Gay Male Leather 1962–1997." In *Reclaiming San Francisco: History, Politics, Culture,* edited by James Brook, Chris Carlsson, and Nancy Peters, 247–72. San Francisco: City Lights.

Ruedi, Katerina, Sarah Wigglesworth, and Duncan McCorquodale, eds. 1996. *Desiring Practices: Architecture, Gender, and the Interdisciplinary.* London: Black Dog.

Ryan, Jenny, and Hilary Fitzpatrick. 1996. "The Space That Difference Makes: Negotiation and Urban Identities Through Consumption Practices." In *From the Margins to the Centre: Cultural Production and Consumption in the Post-industrial City,* edited by J. O'Connor and D. Wynne, 169–201. Aldershot, England: Arena.

Schrift, Alan D. 1995. "Reconfiguring the Subject as a Process of the Self: Following

Foucault's Nietzschean Trajectory to Butler, Laclau/Mouffe, and Beyond." *New Formations* 25 (summer): 28–39.

Scott, J. W. 1993. "The Evidence of Experience." In *The Lesbian and Gay Studies Reader,* edited by Henry Abelove, Michele A. Barale, and David M. Halperin, 397–415. London: Routledge.

Sedgwick, Eve. 1990. *Epistemology of the Closet.* New York: Harvester Wheatsheaf.

———. 1994. "Queer and Now." In *Tendencies,* 1–20. London: Routledge.

Seebohm, K. 1992. "Contested Terrain in the Urban Landscape: Homosexual Space in Inner-city Sydney." Paper delivered at the inaugural Joint New Zealand Geographical and Australian Institute of Geographers Conference, January, Auckland, New Zealand.

Seidman, Steven. 1998. "Are We All in the Closet? Notes Towards a Sociological and Cultural Turn in Queer Theory." *European Journal of Cultural Studies* 1: 177–92.

Sennett, Richard. 1991. *The Conscience of the Eye: The Design and Social Life of Cities.* London: Faber and Faber.

———. 1994. *Flesh and Stone: The Body and the City in Western Civilization.* London: Faber and Faber.

Sibley, David. 1995. *Geographies of Exclusion.* London and New York: Routledge.

Silverstein, C., and E. White. 1973. *The Joy of Gay Sex: An Intimate Guide for Gay Men to the Pleasures of a Gay Lifestyle.* New York: Crown.

Simmel, Georg. 1971. "Fashion." In *On Individuality and Social Forms,* edited by G. Wills and D. Midgely, 102–24. Chicago: Univ. of Chicago Press.

Sinclair, Iain. 1991. *Downriver.* London: Granta.

———. 1997. *Lights Out for the Territory: 9 Excursions in the Secret History of London.* London: Granta.

Skeggs, Beverley. 1997. *Formations of Class and Gender.* London: Sage.

Sontag, Susan. 1983. "The Fascination of Fascism." In *The Susan Sontag Reader,* 305–25. London: Penguin.

Spoonley, P. 1993. *Racism and Ethnicity.* Auckland: Oxford Univ. Press.

Squires, Judith. 1994. "Private Lives, Secluded Places: Privacy as Political Possibility." *Environment and Planning D: Society and Space* 12: 387–401.

Stanley, Christopher. 1993. "Sins and Passions." *Law and Critique* 4: 207–26.

Stokes, Evelyn. 1987. "Maori Geography or Geography of Maoris." *The New Zealand Geographer* 43, no. 3: 118–23.

Stone, Sandy. 1991. "The Empire Strikes Back: A Posttransexual Manifesto." In *Body Guards: The Cultural Politics of Gender Ambiguity,* edited by Julia Epstein and Kristina Straub, 280–304. New York: Routledge.

Styles, Joseph. 1979. "Outsider/Insider: Researching Gay Baths." *Urban Life* 8: 135–52.

Swanson, G. 1995. " 'Drunk with Glitter': Consuming Spaces and Sexual Geographies." In *Postmodern Cities and Spaces,* edited by Sophie Watson and Kathy Gibson, 80–98. Oxford: Blackwell.

Titmuss, Richard. 1974. *Social Policy.* London: Allen and Unwin.

Travers, A. 1993. "An Essay on Self and Camp." *Theory, Culture, and Society* 10: 127–43.

Troiden, R. 1974. "Homosexual Encounters in a Highway Rest Stop." In *Sexual Deviance and Sexual Deviants,* edited by E. Goode and R. Troiden, 211–28. New York: Morrow.

Tyler, Carol-Anne. 1994. "Passing: Narcissism, Identity, and Difference." *Differences: A Journal of Feminist Cultural Studies* 6, nos. 2–3: 212–48.

Valentine, Gill. 1992. "Out of Sight, Out of Mind: A Geography of a Lesbian Community." Paper presented at the Sexuality and Space Network Conference, "Lesbian and Gay Geographies?" September, London.

————. 1993a. "(Hetero)sexing Space: Lesbian Perceptions and Experiences of Everyday Space." *Environment and Planning D: Society and Space* 11: 395–413.

————. 1993b. "Negotiating and Managing Multiple Sexual Identities: Lesbian Time-Space Strategies." *Transactions of the Institute of British Geographers* 18: 237–48.

————. 1996. "(Re)negotiating the 'Heterosexual Street': Lesbian Productions of Space." In *BodySpace,* edited by Nancy Duncan, 146–55. London and New York: Routledge.

Van Gelder, Lindsey, and Pamela Robin Brandt. 1992. *Are You Two . . . Together? A Gay and Lesbian Travel Guide to Europe.* London: Virago.

Vidler, Anthony. 1992. *The Architectural Uncanny: Essays in the Modern Unhomely.* Cambridge, Mass.: MIT Press.

Waikato Times. 1992. "Pregnant Man Thrilled to Be Giving Birth." May 27, 1.

Walker, Lisa. 1993. "How to Recognize a Lesbian: The Cultural Politics of Looking Like What You Are." *Signs: A Journal of Women in Culture and Society* 18, no. 4: 866–90.

Weightman, Barbara. 1980. "Gay Bars as Private Places." *Landscape Research* 23: 9–16.

Weston, Kath. 1995. "Get Thee to a Big City: Sexual Imaginary and Great Gay Migration." *GLQ* 2: 253–77.

White, Edmund. 1986. *States of Desire: Travels in Gay America.* London: Picador.

————. 1995. "Sado-machismo." 1979. Reprinted in *The Burning Library: Writings on Art, Politics, and Sexuality 1969–1993,* 56–66. London: Picador.

Wigley, Mark. 1992. "Untitled: The Housing of Gender." In *Sexuality and Space,* edited by Beatriz Colomina, 327–89. New York: Princeton Architectural Press.

Wilson, Elizabeth. 1985. *Adorned in Dreams: Fashion and Modernity.* London: Virago.

————. 1992. "Fashion and the Meaning of Life." *The Guardian,* May 18, 34.

Wilson, N. C. 1994. *Women in Sport: Exercise and Pregnancy.* Dunedin, Scotland: School of Physical Education, University of Otago.

Winchester, H. P. M., and P. E. White. 1988. "The Location of Marginalised Groups in the Inner City." *Environment and Planning D: Society and Space* 6, no. 1: 37–54.

Woodhead, David. 1995. " 'Surveillant Gays': HIV, Space, and the Constitution of Identities." In *Mapping Desire: Geographies of Sexualities,* edited by David Bell and Gill Valentine, 231–44. London: Routledge.

Wright, Elizabeth. 1992. *Feminism and Psychoanalysis: A Critical Dictionary.* Oxford: Blackwell.

Wright, Patrick. 1991. *A Journey Through Ruins: The Last Days of London.* London: Verso.

Young, Iris Marion. 1988. "The Exclusion of Women from Sport: Conceptual and Existential Dimensions." In *Philosophic Inquiry in Sport,* edited by W. J. Morgan and K. V. Meier, 211–45. Leeds: Human Kinetics.

———. 1990a. *Justice and the Politics of Difference.* Princeton: Princeton Univ. Press.

———. 1990b. "The Scaling of Bodies and the Politics of Identity." In *Justice and the Politics of Difference,* 122–55. Princeton: Princeton Univ. Press.

———. 1990c. *Throwing Like a Girl and Other Essays in Feminist Philosophy and Social Thought.* Indianapolis: Indiana Univ. Press.

Index

147

consumption, 48
Core, P., 124
cottaging, 89
couvade syndrome, 8
Crawford, S., 12
Cream, J., 2–3
Crimp, D., 105, 106
cross-dressing, 62
cruising zone, 107
cultural differences, 9
cultural tagging, 45
cyberspace, 98

de Beauvoir, S., 68
Debord, G., 119
deconstructive critique, 39
Defiant Pose, 120
Deleuze G., 78
Deleuze and Guattari, 119
Derrida, J., 39, 77, 78
designer labels, 59
detournement, 120–22
Different City for a Different Life (Constant),
    100
displacement, 83
domestic space, 95, 96
Douglas, M., 50; and Isherwood, B., 30, 35,
    45
Duggan, L., 60

England 8, 113, 115–28
equal opportunities policies, 75
Essentially Speaking (Fuss), 36
Expectant Mother (New Zealand
    Obstetrical and Gynaecological
    Society), 12

fashion, 57–59
feminism, 31, 37, 68, 70; theory of, 61;
    writers and, 120
fertility treatment, 6

FHM, 59
Fisher, Dr. R., 6
Fitzpatrick, H., and Ryan, J., 86, 88
Flesh and Stone (Sennett), 81
Folsom Street (San Francisco), 113
Foreign Bodies (Lingis), 101
Foster, J., 74
Foucauldian sense, 81
Foucault, M., 3, 58, 70, 76
Fraser, M., 69, 72
Freud, S., 82
Frye, M. 69
Fuss, D., 36

Gardner, C. B., 4
Gatens, M., 4
Gay Men Fighting AIDS (GMFA), 92
Gay Skins (Healy), 122
Gay Village (Manchester), 113
gays: and bars, 85–87; and chauvinism,
    112; and consumption, 104; and
    geographies, 43; and ghettoes, 84; icons
    of, 74; male, 40, 41, 104; male nurse, 65;
    nonghetto, 94; and press, 98; and
    suburbia, 93
gaze, 91
Gender Trouble (Butler), 61
gentrification, 104
geography: of lesbians, 39–40; Māori, 34;
    transport 97
Germany, 7
Giddens, A., 58
Golding, S., 101, 127
GQ, 59
Grahn, J., 31
Grant, A., and Chouinard, V., 31
Grosz, E., 20, 77
group categorization, 32
Guattari, F., and Deleuze, G., 119

Hallam, P., 108
Hamilton (New Zealand), 1–2